Arts and International Affairs

Also from Westphalia Press
westphaliapress.org

Arts and International Affairs

Arts and Cultural Institutions

Volume 2, Number 3
Autumn/Winter 2017

J. P. Singh, Editor
Evangelos Chrysagis, Managing Editor

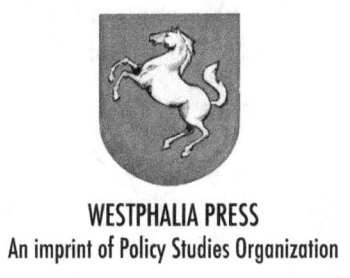

WESTPHALIA PRESS
An imprint of Policy Studies Organization

Arts and International Affairs: Vol. 2, No.3, Autumn/Winter 2017

Westphalia Press
An imprint of Policy Studies Organization
1527 New Hampshire Ave., NW
Washington, D.C. 20036
info@ipsonet.org

ISBN-13: 978-1-63391-673-9
ISBN-10: 1-63391-673-1

Cover and interior design by Jeffrey Barnes:
jbarnesbook.design

Daniel Gutierrez-Sandoval, Executive Director
PSO and Westphalia Press

Updated material and comments on this edition
can be found at the Westphalia Press website:
www.westphaliapress.org

ARTS AND CULTURAL INSTITUTIONS

Our Longform articles are double-blind peer reviewed.
The Brushstrokes and Multimedia articles undergo
an extensive in-house editorial process.

EDITORIAL: ARTS AND CULTURAL INSTITUTIONS

J.P. SINGH

The University of Edinburgh

> J.P. Singh is Professor and Chair of Culture and Political Economy, and Director of the Institute for International Cultural Relations at the University of Edinburgh.

This issue of *Arts & International Affairs* explores the connections between art and cultural institutions. Arts are symbolic practices and reflect on ways of life. Institutions are formal repositories for experiences, learning, and conventions. While obviously related, arts and cultural institutions are not the same and this issue of AIA explores the synergies and divergences.

Arts are creative and they are cultural. A creative experience is part of the artists' imagination, pursued both with talent and genius. Creative practices become cultural when they reflect, or are embodied in, collective beliefs and experiences (Singh 2011). Equally they can question cultural practices and the arts have often pushed this boundary. Despite all the controversies, and the groups that are marginalized or included, each year's arts' awards—whether for books or films or fine arts—celebrate those who pushed the boundaries of our thinking and told a story that needed to be heard in ways we had not imagined before. The social world of art often either romanticizes the renegade who defected from cultural practices or revels in one controversy or another: the Ukrainian ballet dancer Sergei Polunin who in 2012 announced his resignation from the Royal ballet at the age of 22 at the height of his career; Bollywood's *Padmavaat* in 2017–2018 that ignited controversies with far-right Hindu nationalists for its portrayal of an apocryphal Hindu Princess; or a January 2018 production of the opera Carmen in Florence, which changed the ending for a feminist close in which the opera's eponymous heroine kills Don José rather than the other way around—the audiences booed the production, the Mayor of Florence defended it.

Cultural institutions also shape artistic practices, and can embody the political economies of their time, in turn constraining or regulating art. Social scientists have shown that arts and cultural institutions should stand at an arms-length from political processes in order to encourage a diversity and freedom of artistic expressions (Throsby 2000; Frey 2000). Thus, a ministry of culture controlling arts funding is very different from a National Endowment for the Arts in the United States or the Arts Council England. On the other hand, the problem is that arts regulators and funding agencies do not passively reflect a "public interest" and have internal prerogatives (Rizzo 2003). There are also macro political-economies that arts embroil, inviting charges of reflecting particular ideologies and taste (Miller and Yúdice 2002). While artistic practices shape arts agencies, more often the latter are risk-averse and conservative despite an occasional controversy.

This issue highlights many tensions and confluences between arts and cultural institutions. We present two themes: one dealing with the 'Status of (Inter)National Organizations as Cultural Institutions,' and the other titled 'Cities, Culture, and the Proliferation of the Biennials.' Our new Managing Editor, Evangelos Chrysagis, is to be credited for creating these sub-themes.

'Status of (Inter)National Organisations at Cultural Institutions' deals both with the limits and the possibilities of arts and cultural institutions. Scholar Naomi Adiv's forceful piece notes that the threat to the cut-off less than $150 million in annual funding for the National Endowment for the Arts in the United States has less to do with budget savings—it's an infinitesimal part of the federal budget—but with broad conservative grudges and "culture war tropes" that seek limit government involvement in the arts or curtailing particular types of arts expressions. Across the Atlantic Ocean, the British Council presents a contrasting story. Director of Arts Graham Sheffield writes to the power of theater in cultivating the British Council's agenda of fostering cultural relations among communities and nations. Rather than avoiding controversial issues, the British Council has sometimes dealt with them headlong and with reflection. For example, last year the British Council sponsored a production of Argentine Director Lola Arias' Minefield exploring the 1982 Falklands/Malvinas war not based on the politics of the Argentine or the UK but from the perspective of the war's personal tolls and horrors. The British Council is part of the UK government's soft power strategy but even as a quasi-government cultural relations organisation it has sometimes not shied away from taking on difficult subjects and it is certainly not immune to funding cuts. There was some opposition to funding Minefield within the British government.

The Mafalda Dâmaso article shows how art may expose the limits of an organisation's ideals, in this case that of the United Nations, through art. She describes Pedro Reyes 2013–2014 exhibit titled *The People's United Nations*. Dâmaso's theoretical exhumation of the project shows how the UN is far from its ideals of democracy and deliberation.

Our second theme is 'Cities, Culture, and the Proliferation of Biennials.' All three essays are aware of the importance of the creative economies and tourist monies generated through cultural events such as the biennales and the growing cultural importance of cities. Scholars Julia Bethwaite and Anni Kangas, nevertheless, explore not just the dominance of nation-states or the market modes of production inherent in the nearly 150 arts biennials in more than 50 countries. They also show how the biennials foster resistance, diversity, and creativity. Similarly, Anne Murray's multi-media interview with the two curators and co-founders of the Mediterranean Biennial of Contemporary Art of Oran, Algeria, posits the value of this biennial along with the value and dominance of Venice Biennale across the Mediterranean. Certainly, co-curators Sadek Rahim and Tewfik

Ali Chaaouche are aware of the tremendous creativity in Oran but also of the 8 million tourists who visit the city annually. The theme of how cities prepare for presentation as cultural sites and tourism is taken up in Anna Lisa Boni and Philippe Kern's article. The authors are European cultural officials and practitioners. Their practical advice for the cultural preparedness of cities includes a note on the cosmopolitanism of city cultural workers.

In the perennial debate on whether art shapes cultural institutions or vice versa, this issue of *Arts & International Affairs* seems to offer a somewhat safe answer betwixt the perspectives. But the authors venture beyond safety in noting the boundaries and provocations where art challenges cultural institutions, or where it reflects the prerogatives of institutions but also provides resistance and redefinition. We invite your indulgence!

References

Frey, Bruno S. (2003) *Arts and Economics: Analysis and Cultural Policy*. Berlin: Springer.

Miller, Toby and George Yúdice. (2002) *Cultural Policy*. Thousand Oaks, CA: Sage.

Rizzo, Ilde. (2003) Regulation. In *A Handbook of Cultural Economics*, ed. Ruth Towse, 408–414. Cheltenham, UK: Edward Elgar.

Singh, J.P. (2011) *Globalized Arts: The Entertainment Economy and Cultural Identity*. New York, NY: Columbia University Press.

Throsby, David. (2010) *The Economics of Cultural Policy*. Cambridge: Cambridge University Press.

THE BRITISH COUNCIL AND THE POWER OF THEATRE[1]

GRAHAM SHEFFIELD CBE

Graham Sheffield has been Global Director Arts for the British Council since 2011. He is responsible for leading the worldwide arts strategy and programme across the British Council's 116 country operation. From 1995–2010 Graham was Artistic Director of the Barbican Centre in London. Under his directorship, the Barbican developed into one of the most innovative, dynamic and respected arts centres, with an award-winning international programme across the arts spectrum. In the last six years he has driven a major expansion and reshaping of the arts programme at the British Council, defining a new vision, developing new arts specialists in the global network, planning major extended seasons of work in Brazil, China, Qatar, India, Mexico, Nigeria, Russia, Korea and South Africa, as well as responding ambitiously to social and political change in the Middle East, Gulf, North Africa and South Asia. Under Graham's leadership, the arts programme has grown in size and impact, and has attracted significant investment and partner funding: to launch a Cultural Skills programme, expand the work within the Creative Industries sector, develop a digital arts programme and refresh and enlarge the British Council's internationally renowned Art Collection—a vital contributor to work overseas in cultural relations. A recent development is leading a £30m Cultural Protection Fund on behalf of the ministry to help protect important world heritage sites under threat. Also, he has introduced the Council's first ever post in computer games. Graham graduated in Music from Edinburgh University and worked as a Radio 3 producer at the BBC for 12 years on classical music, opera, features and documentaries. From there he moved to the Southbank Centre as Music Projects Director for 5 years, founding the world-renowned Meltdown Festival in 1993. He also served as CEO of the West Kowloon Cultural District, Hong Kong in 2010. He was Chair of the Royal Philharmonic Society (2007–2010), and consulted to the new Luminato Festival of Arts and Creativity in Toronto. From 2004–2006 Graham was Chair of the International Society of Performing Arts and a council member of Arts Council England, London (2002–2008). In 2014 Graham took up a new role as Chair of the UK's largest music charity, Help Musicians UK and joined the Board of Rambert. He was awarded CBE in the 2010 New Year's Honours' list for services to the arts and was made Chevalier de l'ordre des Arts et des Lettres by the

---

[1] Editor's Note: This is an edited version of the speech delivered by Graham Sheffield for the opening of the National Taichung Theater, Taiwan on 1st October 2016.

French government in 2005. He is an honorary Doctor of Arts at City University, and a fellow of the Royal Society of Arts. Graham was honoured in January 2015 by ISPA with the International Citation of Merit for lifetime achievement in the arts.

The British Council was set up in 1934 as a response to the rise of Fascism in Europe: it achieved its independent charter (at arm's length from government) in 1940, and the mission from that year still resonates, as we strive "to create a friendly knowledge and understanding between the peoples of the UK and the wider world", by making a positive contribution to the (now) 115 countries we work in, and in doing so making a lasting difference to the UK's international standing, prosperity and security. In short, though the term is not one I am drawn to, we are in effect the UK's instrument of "soft power". (I feel that "soft power" rather diminishes the impact—even though I realise what is meant.)

Theatre became an important part of the British Council's mission in the immediate aftermath of World War Two. We were eager to return to Europe (strange turnaround from just over half the UK now that wants "out" of Europe—another topic, another day!), and by the mid-1940s had reopened many of our former offices closed during the conflict and extended into new countries for us, such as France and Austria. In a continent fractured by extreme ideologies and huge loss of life, the British Council set about disseminating British culture. In the years immediately after the war, the Sadler's Wells Ballet Company visited Paris, Ghent, Brussels, Vienna, Prague, Warsaw, Poznan, Malmo and Oslo. And under the auspices of Laurence Olivier, Ralph Richardson and Sybil Thorndike, the Old Vic Theatre Company went to Paris, Brussels, Australia and New Zealand. In her history of the British Council, Frances Donaldson remarked "*it is doubtful the British taxpayer is, or ever has been, aware of how much he owes these two companies in international renown*". Over the same period, the British Council was instrumental in the creation of the first Edinburgh International Festival in 1947. Today of course, the Edinburgh Festivals are the world's largest arts festivals and a bulwark of the Scottish economy.

These days the work of the British Council, across the spectra of English language learning, higher education, civil society and the arts, is about a lot more than simply "showcasing" the best of British, whether in theatre or in any of the myriad of art forms we work in: our own kind of Wagnerian gesamtkunstwerk, if you like! We don't act as a touring agency for one thing; most of our work is done in partnership with others, convening, connecting, yes funding too, but in a much more nuanced way, looking at cultural relations as of genuinely mutual and reciprocal benefit.

With all the turbulence and uncertainty in the world today, it's arguable that the role of the arts, and theatre in particular, is even more important to any country's engagement in international relations—the UK in particular, since our creative sector is so strong.

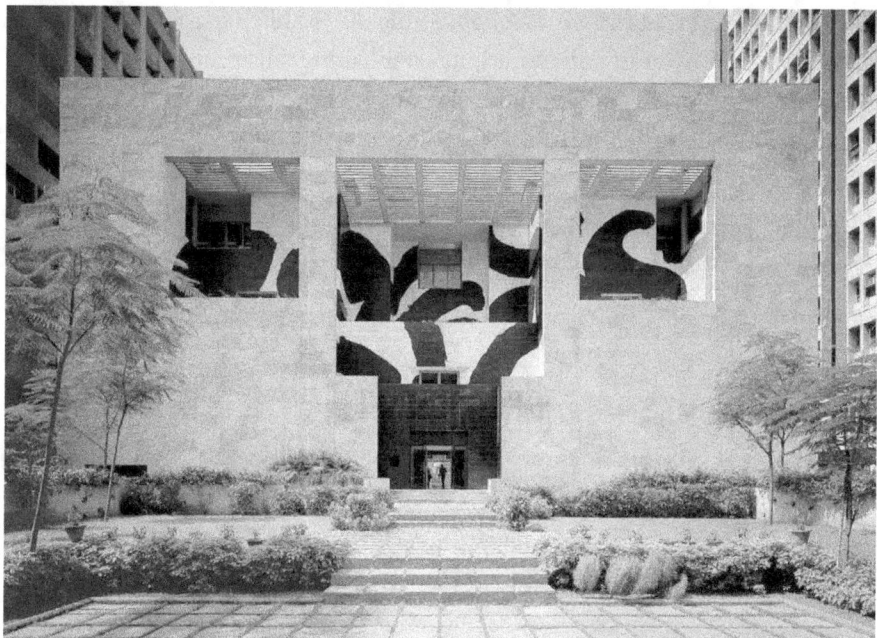

Figure 1: British Council Building in New Delhi, India

When I started at the British Council, I soon saw that we needed to amplify the work we were doing across the arts—but again, particularly in theatre—to make a difference in society, in effect to advance the cause of social change. This wasn't and isn't about crude instrumentalism, it is about acknowledging (as we've been discussing) that theatre has a power, has an impact in the social arena to create a platform for positive social change—in attitudes to women, to racism, to intolerance of minorities, to health and well-being.

To my mind, artists in the UK are more engaged in such fields than at any time since the late 1960s—more "up for" direct social engagement on the pressing issues of the day through drama and the arts. And as the UK's international cultural relations organization, my colleagues and I thought it is imperative that we expanded our remit beyond showcasing into these more challenging and controversial areas.

In the deployment of theatre in such matters, it's most often about attempting to change people's attitudes within a so-called safe space, catalysing change in individuals through the directness and emotional power of the work. As my colleague in New Zealand, Ingrid Leary, said in relation to the project "Stages of Change" she is directing in theatre in the Solomon Islands, tackling crippling issues of domestic violence towards women: "the key was inspiration through theatre, not just informing in a workshop setting, so that the impact was lived with and absorbed, rather than just learned."

The project, much respected for the changes it has brought, addressed not only women's issues but also broad cultural taboos—sexual, gender and religious. It raised awareness, which led to behaviour change. And it was led by a local Melanesian (not imposed from outside), which meant that the women could quickly establish trust, and grow their own confidence. It was a power of collaboration, establishing a listening environment, a safe space. The theatre was "physical" with local props (echoes of Artaud here), so there was a low risk of mistranslation or misunderstanding.

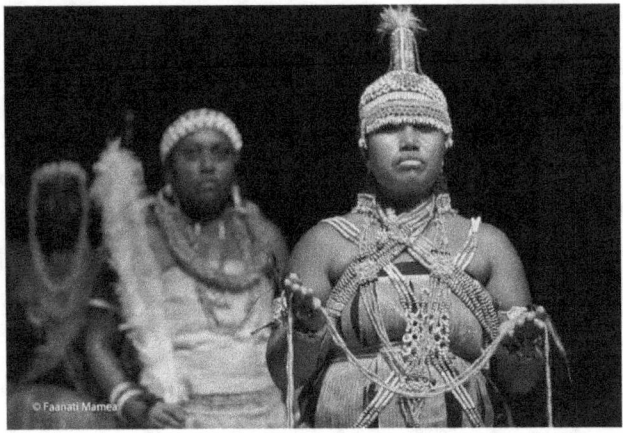

Figure 2: Stages of Change, Solomon Islands

Evidence of policy change also comes from that project: women now are seen and heard more in public, and the project is credited by the EU funders for having contributed to new legislation—the Solomon's Family Protection Act 2014. Ingrid also considers it important in increased international connectivity for the Solomon Islands government in the South Pacific. Several women have visited other Pacific Festivals and stages.

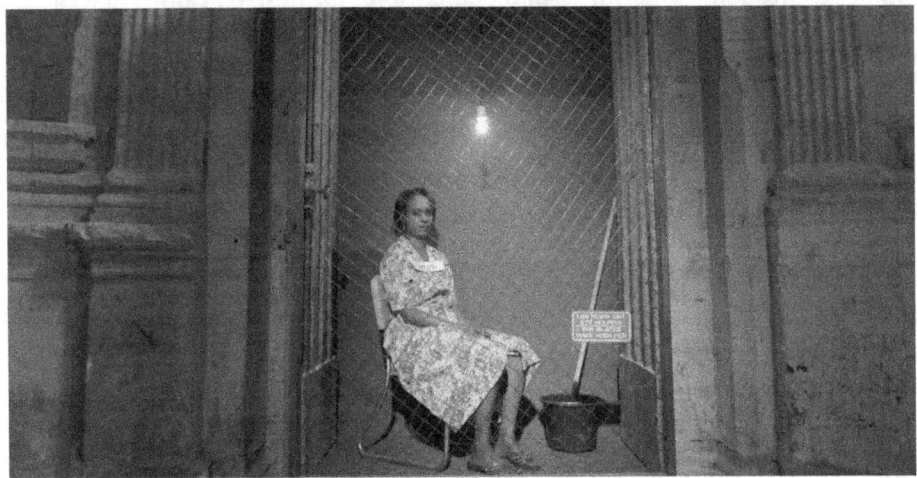

Figure 3: Exhibit B, Brett Bailey

Theatre is a place to open up discussions about identity, history and race. Take Exhibit B, a live art/theatre installation created by white South African director Brett Bailey, with his multi-talented and multi-racial cast. It was a unique hybrid of performance and exhibition, looking at themes of racism and Europe's colonial history through a startling set of 13 fixed installations peopled by the brave cast.

I saw it in the elegant surroundings of Edinburgh University's old library, a noble architectural articulation of eighteenth-century Enlightenment philosophy, somewhat at odds with the challenging material ... decidedly NON-enlightened! It was a powerful combination, and one which had received plaudits, as well (yes) as sparking debate. I found it unbearably moving, especially considering the roles willingly taken on by the enterprising cast.

It was based on the concept of "human zoos" and ethnographic displays popularised (not SO long ago) at the end of the nineteenth century. In each tableau, the audience (who see it in small numbers, walking around as if IN a museum) is confronted by a black performer, who casts an unsettling, silent gaze upon the viewer. Utterly compelling! The reviews used words such as "moving, vital, disturbing, unbearable, essential" not only as a political statement relating to the past and European guilt but also as a compelling piece of theatre.

Imagine my dismay and anger when it was prevented from opening at the Barbican (my former venue) later in 2014 by a group of ill-informed protestors, using violence and threats. I was particularly angered, since I had worked so hard at the Barbican to build its reputation for progressive international theatre—as well as presenting several excellent shows by Brett Bailey. The protestors (who hadn't even seen it!) called it an act of "complicit racism", which was about as stupid a criticism as you could invent—it was precisely the opposite! And they had no right to prevent other free-minded adults from seeing it, judging it and responding to it. A shameful episode all round: bad for freedom of expression, bad for the Barbican's reputation, unfortunate for Bailey and his cast. But you can't deny THAT piece of theatre packs a powerful punch, whichever side you are on.

Theatre also has a role in empowering marginalised groups. According to figures from the UN High Commissioner for Refugees (UNHCR), the conflict in Syria has forced almost five million people to leave their homes and seek refuge in other countries. The majority of these are women and children, living in neighbouring countries, with little prospect of returning home in the near future. In 2013, Refuge Productions brought together 60 Syrian refugee women living in Jordan to adapt and perform Euripides' anti-war tragedy, The Women of Troy, as well as Antigone by Sophocles. The director was Syrian and they worked with an Egyptian author in a contemporary version of the stories.

We also supported them through the British Council, and I was privileged to meet some of them at a regional arts meeting in Beirut a year ago, and see documentary footage of some of their work. They'd never acted before, and the extraordinary piece of theatre they produced weaves together their own stories of life as refugees and their experience of war and terrible loss with the ancient Greek text.

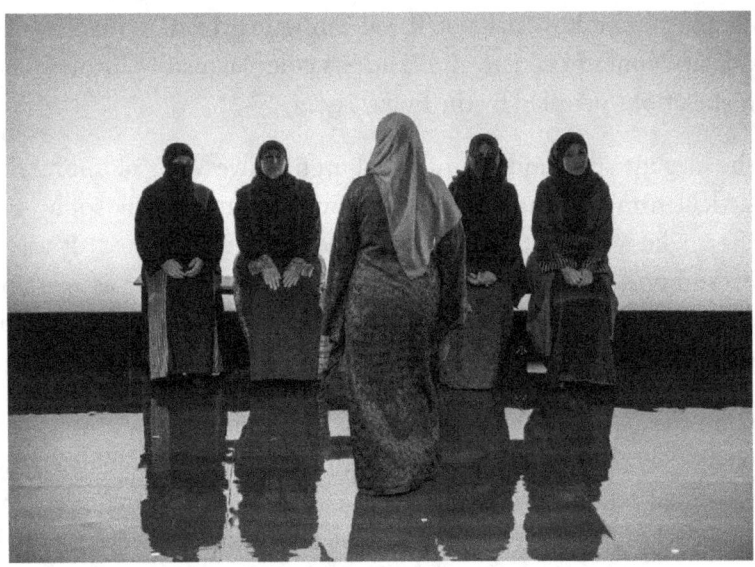

Figure 4: The Syrian Trojan Women Project

One of them said to me "the brother (Polynices) buried outside the walls of Thebes without a proper funeral in Antigone is MY brother—that's what the drama means to me". So these were real people inserted, as it were, into an ancient drama, as if part of yourself was inhabiting the old story—that story was a framework for their narrative ... a somehow cathartic experience for each of them. They weren't acting ... for them it was real!

The women spoke too of how their theatre work—culturally very unusual for a Muslim woman, changed forever how their husbands and families saw them ... sometimes for the better, sometimes not. But they felt emancipated: that was the important factor.

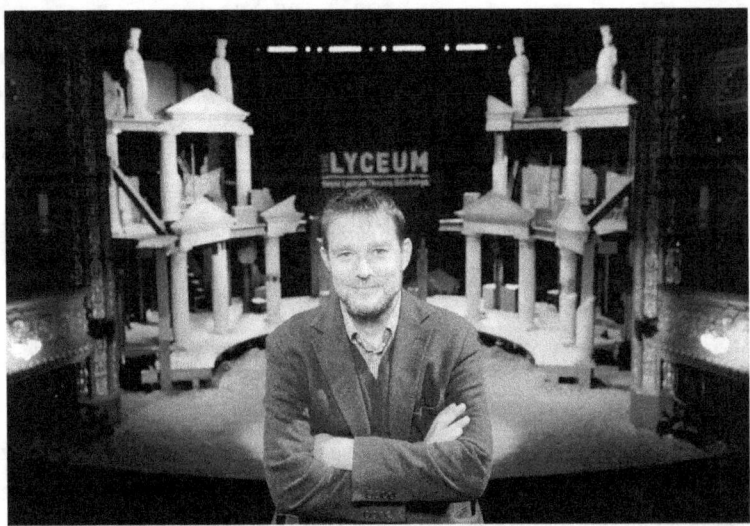

Figure 5: David Greig, Artistic Director of the Royal Lyceum Theatre

In a similar vein, David Greig returned to Aeschylus autumn of 2017 at the Lyceum Theatre in Edinburgh. He's directed a new version of Aeschylus's *The Suppliant Women* (with an amateur community group and reconstituted authentic Greek Aulos music).[2] It was a chillingly familiar tale of refugee women seeking political asylum in Greece from war in the Middle East—who says history doesn't repeat itself?!

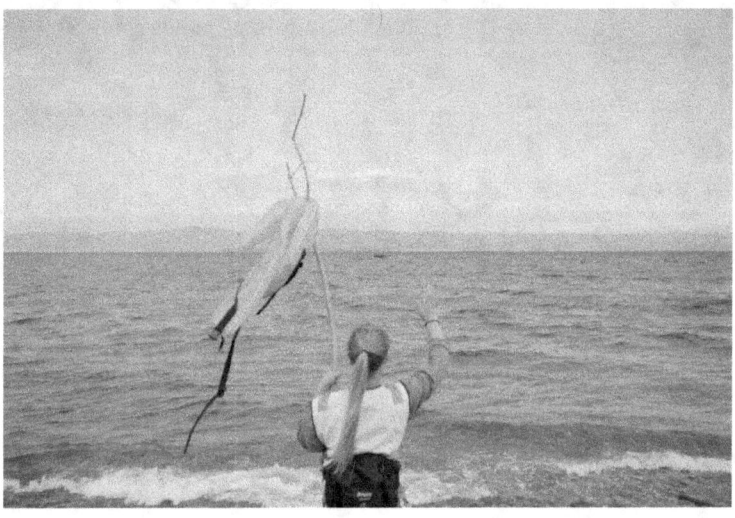

Figure 6: The Suppliant Women, Royal Lyceum Theatre Edinburgh

Theatre can also tackle subjects that are considered "taboo", a bit like my earlier Solomon Islands example. Take a play called Roadkill, about human trafficking, based on the experiences of a young woman trafficked to Scotland from Benin City. It was first produced at the Edinburgh Festival in 2013 and was part of the British Council's Edinburgh Showcase, a biennial platform of contemporary UK performance selected by us and external advisers for the Fringe and ultimately, we hope, for international dates. I'm pleased to say that, as a direct result, the play toured to the US, another country blighted by this serious issue. The performance experience was powerful—an audience of around 25, driven off to a dilapidated house on the outskirts of Edinburgh, installed in a small living room, where the action took place right at your feet. Impossible not to be moved, impossible not to feel empathy, impossible not to emerge with your mind and attitude changed to the plight of such women.

Exploring similar themes was South African director Yael Farber's acclaimed play Nirbhaya—the story of the young Delhi woman who was gang-raped and left for dead. This searing story premiered in Edinburgh a year or so ago and won the coveted Amnesty International Freedom of Expression Award, given to a Fringe show which raises awareness of human rights. We were able to support a tour of Nirbhaya to India, despite nervousness from the UK Foreign Office, and it met with a similar reaction to the global problem of sexual violence: how can societies across the world tackle it?

---

[2] https://www.youtube.com/watch?v=CZZ07U-yOcM

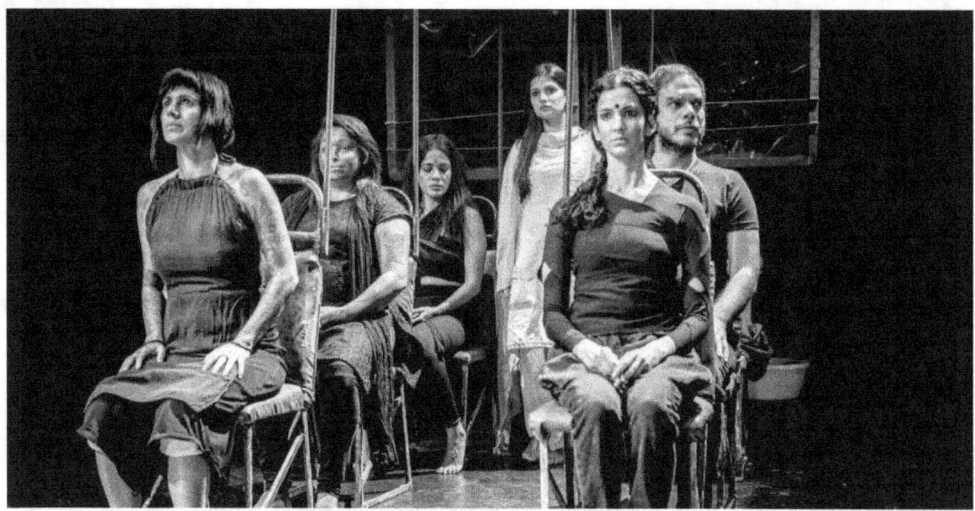

Figure 7: Nirbhaya by Yaël Farber

William Burdett Coutts, the producer, says: "the message behind Nirbhaya is attached to real life". For him, a piece of theatre like this is so much more relevant than yet another version of, say, As You Like It! In Yael's vivid production, "theatre meets church" and leaves something emblazoned on your mind in our ephemeral world. It won't change society overnight, but it keeps on addressing the message in a process of attitudinal change and tolerance.

That's political in a way, and it's difficult to remove yourself from politics in theatre these days. Some directors have more directly engaged with political controversy through the medium of "verbatim" or documentary theatre. One of the finest exponents of this remains Nick Kent, for many years Artistic Director of a small, but radical theatre in North London called the Tricycle.

Perhaps, his greatest achievement (though he has many documentary theatre credits to his name on issues from the Nuremberg Trials to the Srebrenica Massacres) as well as his greatest success was probably around the Great Game, a series of 12 half-hour plays about 170 years of foreign intervention in Afghanistan from 1842 to 2010—from the Anglo-Afghan Wars, through the Russians, the CIA, the coming of the Taliban, Operation "Enduring Freedom, reconstruction, Western aid and the continuing insurgency". It brought together a focus on foreign policy (British, European and American) through political debate and discourse. Premiering in 2009 in London, it then toured the US, even to the Pentagon itself, where it was seen as an educational tool for the US military and officialdom.

Nick has the courage to say that, even though he was against the UK/US invasion at the time, working on the plays led him to change his perspective, in that he came to see that the removal of the Taliban was the lesser of two evils at that time. He's now working on a piece about the radicalisation of young Muslims in Tower Hamlets (a borough in London); even in this, he says that the power of the living research leads him to a deeper understanding of racism in the UK and how it affects society—and has led him to a more tolerant view of Islam. That's power in action if you like: but Nick insists on only using verbatim text, whereas another strongly political British playwright like David Hare adds fiction to the mix to support his view of the situation, which, to my mind, weakens the audience's ability to make up its own mind; it's all too directional.

"Tragic catharsis"—that's what an audience goes through in such drama and with the Greeks. Director and actor Fiona Shaw refers to this as "the rhythm of theatre"—when everything is right, she says, "the heartbeat of the audience matches that of the players, that's what makes theatre unique." As long as the rhythm is correct, it doesn't matter what language it's in—it's the emotion that counts.

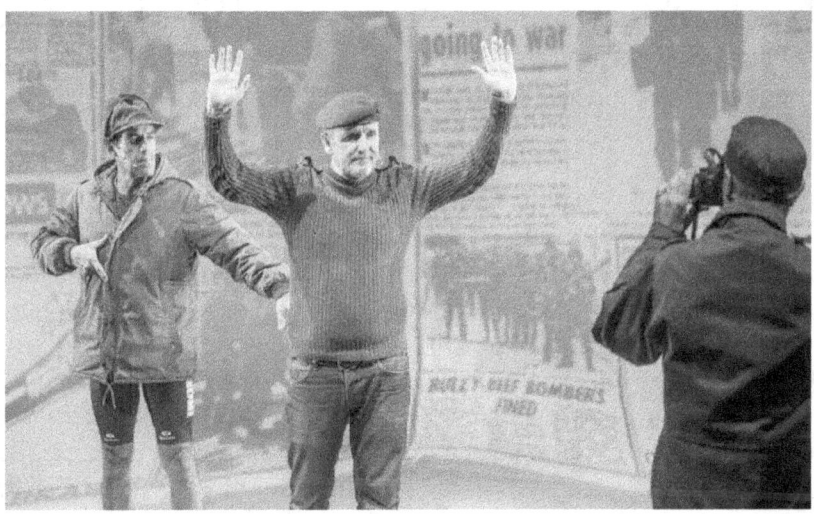

Figure 8: Minefield, Royal Court Theatre, Lift, Brighton Festival

More in line with the Tricycle model was a very recent example, which we were closely involved with relating to the UK's troubled relationship with Argentina—now happily on an upward path. It was called Minefield (an apt title!) and was a developed drama through dialogue and documentary between war veterans from both sides of the Falklands conflict in 1984.[3] It involved a co-commission by the Brighton Festival and London International Festival of Theatre, alongside the Royal Court, and included an experienced Argentinian director, Lola Arias. It wasn't about the contested sovereignty of the islands, but a considered psychological take on the effects of war on combatants and families from both sides, through the lens of the conflict. After the war many got new jobs, as security guards or musicians for example ... and today all they have in common is that they fought each other. Our Foreign Office was initially nervous, but we felt this

---

[3] https://www.youtube.com/watch?v=Xvm9NWr6I4Q

was core to our mission in the arts to build mutual and friendly understanding in areas of difficulty; and our faith was vindicated by the great reception the show received both in the UK and Buenos Aires. It has returned in 2017, to Edinburgh as part of Spirit of 47,[4] as well as on an English regional tour.

The Spirit of 47 programme was a jointly conceived enterprise by the Edinburgh International Festival and the British Council to mark 70 years of the festival and also to mark the involvement of the British Council as one of the founding partners in it back in 1947.[5] The festival was born through the spirit of European reconciliation after World War Two, and as such it was distinctly consonant with the British Council's own mission of building mutual understanding between nations through cultural exchange and collaboration—in this case RE-building. In our jointly curated programme in 2017, we tried to reimagine the festival's founding vision in the context of today's geo-political and social world—global more than merely European, and what the festival might look like if it had been started in 2017, not 1947: the diversity of Europe, the new power of the East, the emergence of new cultural powers. Our programme featured Minefield, almost as a signature statement, but also more than 20 other countries, including Iran, Ukraine, Syria, Palestine and Pakistan.

And recently relations between the UK and Argentina have taken further steps forward—I am convinced that this theatre connection has something directly to do with this, through an increase in mutual trust at a high level. It's not provable, but it definitely represents cultural diplomacy in action through theatre on a challenging subject.

Equally important in changing attitudes is our work (closely with the Southbank Centre in London) on Unlimited, an ongoing programme of work involving disabled artists and creatives. If, as I have, you've been moved by the extraordinary achievements of all the Paralympic athletes in Rio, you will be equally moved by the work of these artists, amongst them choreographer and dancer Clare Cunningham, and writer, artist and play-worker Jess Thom. She co-founded Touretteshero in 2010 to celebrate the humour and creativity of Tourette Syndrome, from which she herself is a sufferer.

Taking on the identity of part-time superhero Touretteshero, she has turned her tics into a source of creative energy to spread the word about this frequently misunderstood neurological condition via a wide range of artistic channels. The company aims to increase awareness of the disorder and its challenges without self-pity or mockery; it makes work that turns the laughter associated with Tourettes into a genuinely funny cultural alternative.

It's this kind of work that Carole McFadden, who has so ably led the programme for us over five years at the British Council, thinks can really change attitudes not only to disability but also to the art forms themselves. Her evidence is the fact that so many

---

[4] https://www.britishcouncil.org/arts/spirit-of-47

[5] https://www.youtube.com/watch?v=rdL68hZPbng&t=38s

international delegates now come to the Unlimited Festival through us—it's now in its third edition at the Southbank, having started as part of the Cultural Olympiad in London in 2012. We are active commissioners and "internationalisers" of the programme with our partners, and Carole has seen her own personal connections with the artists change her. It also leads to policy change and change in attitudes towards access and inclusivity. Now, we are seeing some of the works being programmed not even in a disability context, but in mainstream festival programmes. Progress and power indeed.

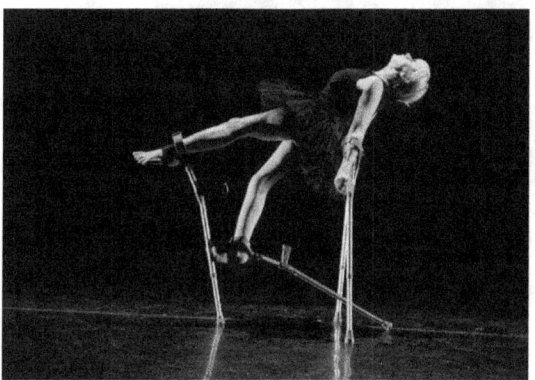 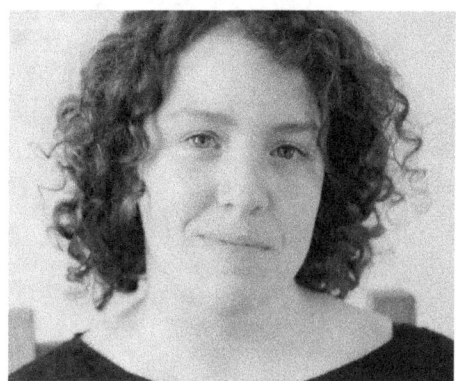

Figure 9: Claire Cunnigham and Jess Thom

National Theatre of Scotland (which works without its own home theatre base) and now director at the world-renowned Royal Court, London's home for new and radical writing … Vicky says: "how little theatre has changed since 400BC. There have been so many challenges to theatre—electricity, television, digital, the challenge of other entertainment, but fundamentally the format hasn't changed. It serves a basic human need, both emotional and intellectual. It presents stories either affirming what we are (a kind of 'hot water bottle' comforter) or those that deconstruct what we are (questioning or disrupting our sense of self). Theatre creates a kind of empathy—we sit as a congregation digesting a narrative. In today's secular world, a world of individual entertainment, with mobile phones, games, the end of family meals and conversation … in such a world theatre (like a concert) is one of the few places we come together to share a story and its impact. We share what someone else is feeling—which is a very sophisticated thing to do. Theatre bears witness to these experiences, and as a member of the audience, they will remain with us for ever, and sometimes produce individual and collective transformation."

I hope you have found some of my examples convincing and powerful—I hope they might have changed and broadened your minds to the potential power of theatre, both emotional and intellectual, to effect change in individuals through a personal transformation and moment.

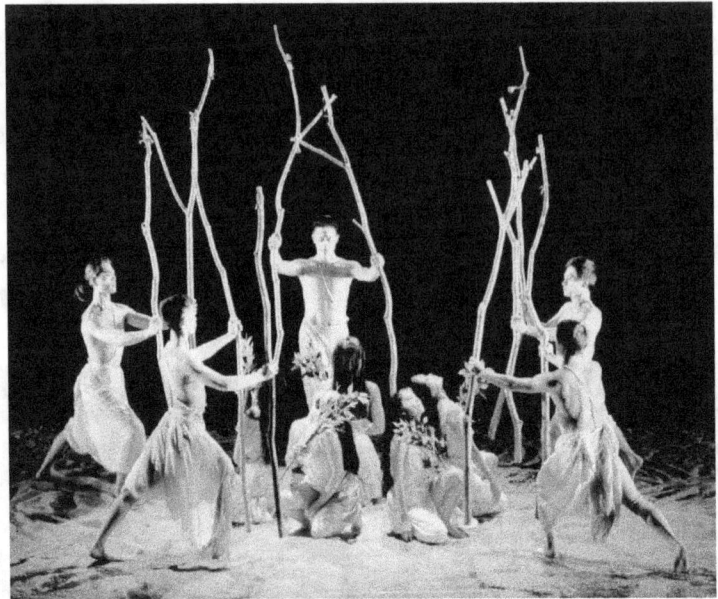

Figure 10: Cloud Gate Dance Theatre performing Rite of Tree

I am left though with that paradox, so neatly and poetically expressed by Lin Hwai Min of Cloud Gate Dance Theatre—I paraphrase him here, for which I hope he'll forgive me. But his essence is that, in this art form, power is expressed both in the moment and in its memory by those who see it. The fact that all we have is "that instant, and those fleeting moments", that evanescent moment is also evidence in the end of theatre's ultimate powerlessness. Powerful or powerless—or both? An endless conundrum! You make up your own mind as you experience your next theatre performance ...

GRAHAM SHEFFIELD: PERSONAL REFLECTIONS

T he essay above records my reflections on the power of theatre from the perspective of the British Council. I work for the British Council—I've been there seven years, after several decades spent in radio and the arts, mostly running multi-arts centres, like the Southbank and the Barbican in London. This short reflective piece collects a few formative experiences that inform my thinking.

In 2016, I was in Liverpool in the north west of England—an old port city, now much revived through investment into the arts, in terms of both its infrastructure and its artists. It's a very cosmopolitan city—birthplace of the Beatles, home to artistic institutions including Tate Liverpool, FACT arts centre, the International Slavery Museum, the Everyman Theatre, as well as Paul McCartney's school for the performing arts. It has a large and diverse population, home to the oldest black and Chinese communities in England, and known historically for its large Irish and Welsh populations. I was there, with most of my arts colleagues from the British Council's East Asia region, for a strategic meeting of the kind we try to hold every year, usually in region, but this time (for the first time) in the UK. The region covers territory from Korea, Japan, China, Taiwan, Hong Kong, down through South East Asia, including Burma, through Indonesia to Australia and New Zealand. This week-long exposure of overseas colleagues to the arts scene in a particular English location, I know, has given them new insight into the power of the arts in urban regeneration in an important city outside of London.

As part of the programme, we invited Professor Geoff Crossick (from the Arts and Humanities Research Council) to talk to us about the value of the arts and his views on evaluation and how we measure it. In his talk to us, one phrase (of many) stuck in my mind: "an impact always starts in the arts with an individual personal experience". It certainly rang true to me, since experiences in the arts—particularly music and theatre—have (I believe) shaped who I am as a human being, who I am as a professional, and my whole persona and emotional make-up over the entirety of my life. It's my artistic "daily bread" as it were, akin to a bowl of rice in the daily diets of most Asian cultures—meals are unthinkable without it! My daily diet for life is unthinkable without some art!

My chosen subject eventually turned out to be Music—I am a trained western classical musician—but I have encountered theatre ever since I was about nine years old, attempting the part of Ariel in Shakespeare's Tempest, dressed in a very fetching mini skirt, which must be one of the earliest theatrical photos of "cross-dressing".

At my senior school, I studied Classics (Latin and Ancient Greek) before switching to Music as a discipline, and in the course of this read, translated and experienced many of the ancient Greek dramas of Aeschylus, Euripides, Sophocles, as well as the comedies—both in English and in an amazing traditional Greek theatre, built at Bradfield

School, where they used to do these dramas IN ancient Greek, and in those days without surtitles.

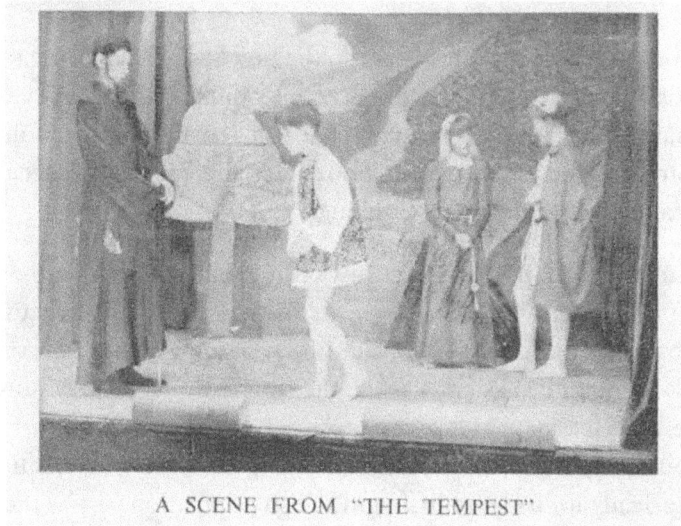

A SCENE FROM "THE TEMPEST"

Figure 11: A "Scene from the Tempest"

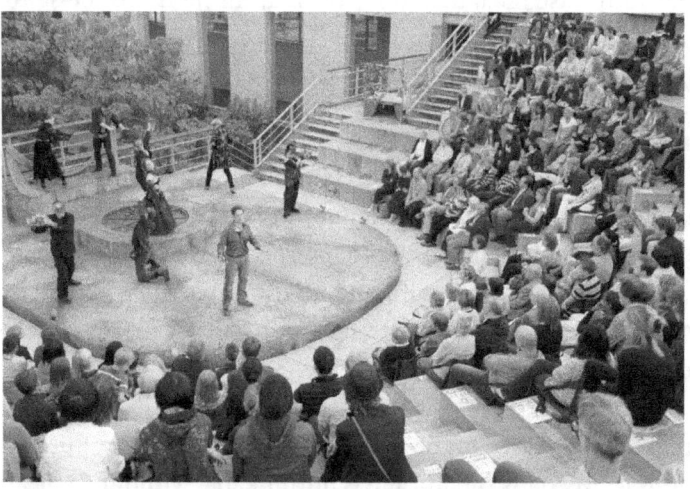

Figure 12: The Greek theatre, Bradfield College

I was hooked very early—by the emotional power of the stories, as well as by the communal nature of the event: a crowd experiencing an ancient story together in a way the Greeks would have done in Epidaurus in 400BC, more than two millennia ago.

I now turn to classic personal influences, particularly the work Brecht, Wagner and Artaud—who although professing different theories—were all attempting to realise the power of theatre through emotional or intellectual frameworks, or a mixture of both.

For Berthold Brecht, theatre was a transformative act, most effective for those who made it, imagining things to become "other". That power he saw almost as shamanic, magic—the power being its roots in ritual. In Brecht's eyes, epic theatre should not cause the spectator actually to identify with the characters or action before them, rather it should provoke a rational self-reflection and a critical view of the action on stage. Brecht, in effect, wanted his audience to adopt a critical perspective in order to recognise social injustice and exploitation, and to be moved to leave the theatre to effect change outside; these techniques reminding the spectator that the play is a representation of reality, not reality itself.

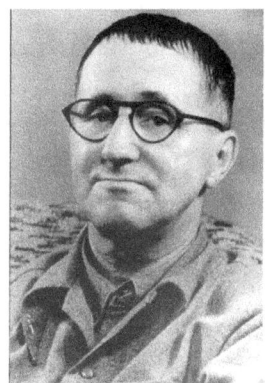 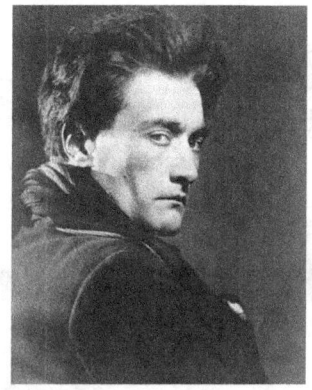 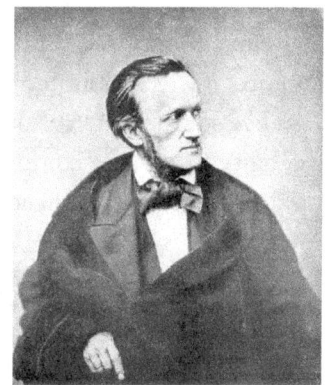

Figure 13: Brecht, Artaud and Wagner

To a large degree, this was the antithesis of the "overwhelming of the senses" advocated by Richard Wagner in his operas, and by the influential dramatist, poet, actor and all round man of the theatre Antonin Artaud.

In 1938, Artaud wrote "Theatre and its Double", a manifesto of his so-called "theatre of cruelty". He sought to create a theatre that was, in effect, a return to magic and ritual, inventing a new theatrical language of totem and gesture, devoid of dialogue, which would appeal to the senses. "Words say little to the mind, compared to space thundering with images and crammed with sounds." Formal theatre with scripts was "a hindrance to the magic of genuine ritual."

Not a million miles away from Wagner almost a century earlier, when in 1849 he coined the term Gesamtkunstwerk—all inclusive art work, embracing and synthesising all the art forms—musical, visual and literary in the interests of an all-powerful sensory experience to overwhelm the spectator.

Wagner was an admirer of the earliest of the Greek dramatists Aeschylus, citing him as the finest exponent of total artistic synthesis, later "corrupted" by Euripides, as the art forms went their separate ways. David Greig's 2017 production of Aeschylus's Suppliant Women, referred to above, was Gesamkunstwerk in the Wagnerian sense.

My perspective on the power of theatre also reflects the work of contemporary directors. One of the European artists I follow most closely (I'm a great admirer of his work) is the Dutch director Ivo van Hove. He would approve of Greig's Suppliant Women, since he feels strongly that theatre can reflect powerfully on politics, especially when there is a distance between current context and the original setting of the play. So, 2,500 years between Aeschylus and the current migration crisis in Europe should do fine! And his own Kings of War (a compelling retelling of Shakespeare's Wars of the Roses plays) was eminently relatable to more recent events on the European political stage. But he is adamant that he seeks no direct change himself: "if you want change," he says, "you'd better go into politics!"

Van Hove thinks that theatre has been declared dead many times. Its resilience to date indicates it will undoubtedly survive the twenty-first century ... a credible power in itself. As a live social event, it fulfils a basic human need, almost unlike any other art form in its ability to create a communal empathy. Issues of society are always deeply rooted in theatre. Bergman said theatre was what made it worthwhile being on this planet.

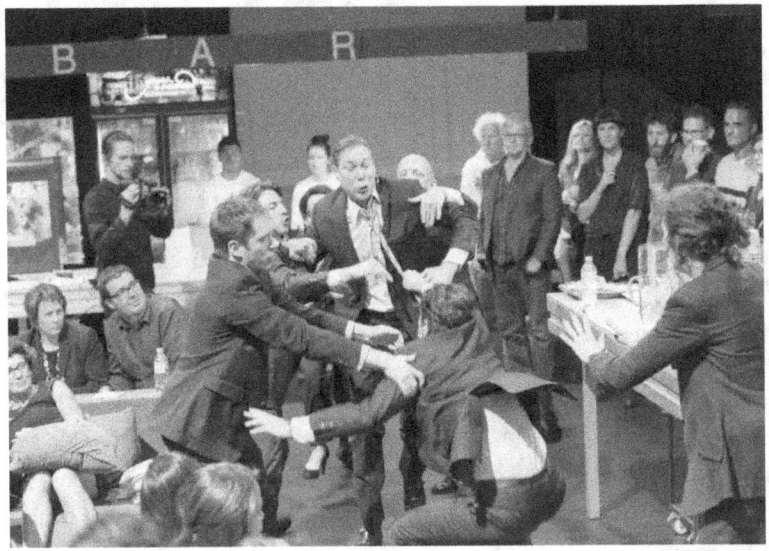

Figure 14: Roman Tragedies, Toneelgoep Amsterdam

Van Hove, though, is more radical when it comes to the audience, looking always to express things in the most extreme way for impact. In his magnificent epic Roman Tragedies (Shakespeare's Coriolanus, Julius Caesar and Anthony and Cleopatra all rolled into one), he cut all the citizen scenes, but effectively recreated the citizenry by allowing the audience to roam on and off the stage, witnessing the action from close-up, framing it and populating it. His theory is based on thoughts on the changing nature of theatre spaces—from open air ten thousand capacity arenas in Greece, to semi open in Shakespeare's day, to semi-private in the nineteenth century, to darkness and individual privacy today. He's, in effect, trying to open it up again ... a theatrical/architectural response, I think to attempt to increase the power—or the communal empathy.

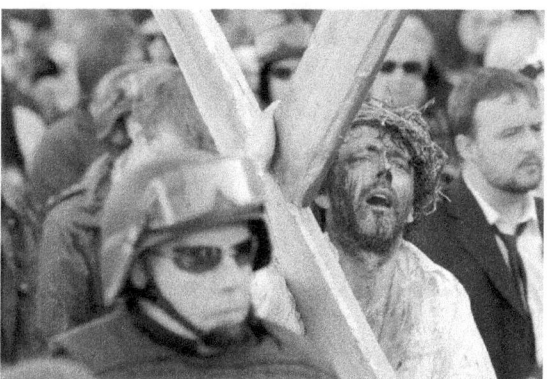

Figure 15: The Passion, National Theatre Wales

John McGrath, director of the Manchester International Festival, formerly the distinguished director of National Theatre Wales, describes his approach to a participating audience somewhat differently. One of the productions from his early time in Wales was called Passion, directed by actor Michael Sheen. It was (to quote the press) a riotous retelling of the biblical crucifixion story, which took place in a depressed steel town in Wales called Port Talbot. The population of the town was the cast. McGrath told me of this communal narrative which everyone shared about the industrial wasteland that was Port Talbot then. The power here manifested itself through the actions of the cast, in particular by the crowd literally shouting at Pontius Pilate, the symbol of Roman authority. For them, he said, they were stepping into a real moment—when narrative becomes reality. A year later, rather than being depressed, the town had begun re-inventing itself, people had begun taking their own futures back.

McGrath thinks theatre the most powerful of art forms, because (unlike music) of the directness of its message. "I wouldn't be in it, if I didn't think it had power."

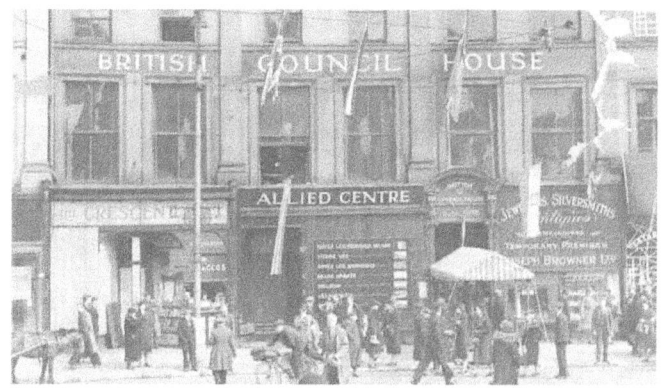

Figure 16: British Council House in the 1930s

ON PEDRO REYES' *THE PEOPLE'S UNITED NATIONS* (2013–2014)—OVERLAPS AND DISJUNCTIONS BETWEEN CONTEMPORARY ART AND INTERNATIONAL AFFAIRS

MAFALDA DÂMASO

Mafalda Dâmaso holds a PhD in Visual Culture from Goldsmiths, University of London. Dâmaso has lectured and worked for several European arts organisations and think tanks, namely as an expert in cultural and foreign policy for the German Institute for Foreign Cultural Relations (Institutfürauslandsbeziehungen). Her research looks at the overlaps between culture, international affairs and rhetoric.

ABSTRACT

This article discusses *The People's United Nations* (2013–2014), a performance and exhibition by the artist Pedro Reyes. Its aim is to understand to what extent artistic practices may constitute a means of critically examining political narratives and hence harbour the potential for the emergence of different forms of responsiveness vis-à-vis international organisations such as the UN. In conversation with key references in political theory (such as Étienne Balibar) and aesthetics (such as Jacques Rancière) as well as a number of related artistic projects, I argue that *The People's United Nations* (2013–2014), which referred to the structure of the General Assembly as its main inspiration, highlighted the limits of the rhetorical claims of the United Nations and the habitual position of the viewer in relation to the organisation, i.e. her lack of involvement. This stressed the hiatus between the UN's official narrative and its modus operandi, foregrounding artistic practice as a possible mode of activated viewership vis-à-vis this international organisation. At the same time, the project's inability to enact its suggestion of institutional reform of the UN also underlined the productive dimension of the partial disjunction between art and international affairs.

Introductory Remarks[1]

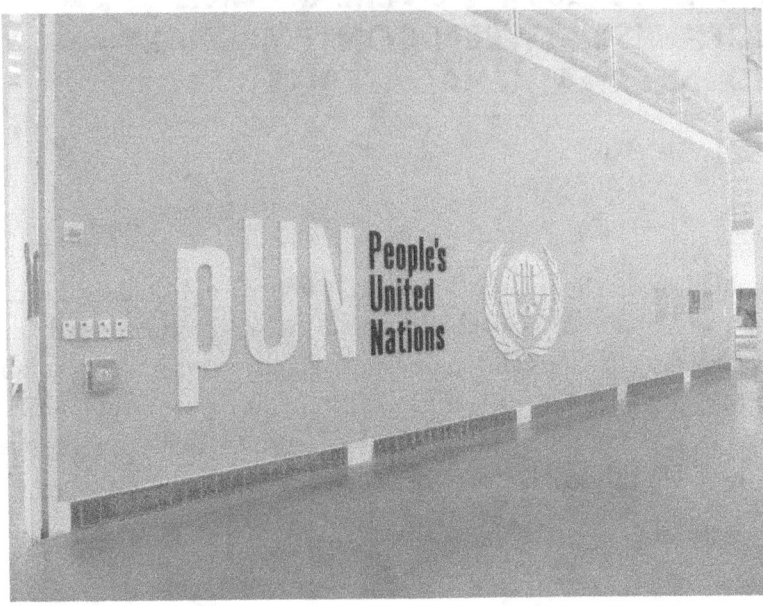

Figure 1: Exhibition view. Courtesy Queens Museum, New York.

A rt and culture scholars tend to agree with the idea that art practices can play a role in expanding ongoing political debates. However, detailed analyses of such a contribution remain rare, especially within the literature on art and international affairs. Indeed, while there are several academic studies of the intersection between art and politics focused on specific regions (e.g. Selz and Landauer 2006; Kane 2013), historical moments (e.g. Frascina 1999; Lobel 2009; Kidd 2014; Golan 1995) and specific types of art practices (e.g. as a form of political resistance in daily life, Clements 2016) or that consider the theoretical underpinnings of the two disciplines (e.g. Harris 2007; Gielen 2015), the overlaps between art and international affairs remain understudied. Among the exceptions to this are publications such as *Designing UNESCO: Art, Architecture and International Politics at Mid-Century,* a historiography of the headquarters of UNESCO (Pearson 2017), as well as discussions on and around soft power (e.g. Watanabe and McConnell 2008; Carles 2016; Nisbett 2016; Lord and Blankenberg 2015) and cultural diplomacy (e.g. Harper 2012; Mikkonen and Suutari 2015; Hampel 2017).

This article aims to contribute to expanding knowledge regarding the intersection between those two fields of knowledge. It does so in a way that is broadly aligned with the

[1] I am thankful to the Portuguese Foundation for Science and Technology for financing my doctoral research, which included part of the analysis presented in this article (Dâmaso 2017). I must also thank Dr Jorella Andrews, Dr Bernadette Buckley, Dr Debbie Lisle and the anonymous reviewer for their insightful comments on an earlier version of this text as well as Pedro Reyes for providing me access to several documents related to *pUN*. Finally, I thank the Queens Museum for allowing me to use images of the project free of charge.

discipline of visual culture[2]—i.e. it considers the engagement by a contemporary artist, Pedro Reyes, with an international institution, the United Nations (UN) by means of the former's appropriation of the latter's visual signs and tropes. This allows me to identify and analyse a set of continuities and lack thereof between the mission of the UN, its institutional framework, the global circulation of its images via mass media, their reception, their artistic appropriation, and the viewership of the latter. *The People's United Nations* (henceforth referred to as *pUN*, 2013–2014)[3] showed that these links are not direct. On the contrary, this art project appropriated and displaced the images and the rhetoric of the UN, inhabiting its inner tensions—namely, regarding the organisation's foundational values of universality, equality and dialogue on the one hand, and its modus operandi on the other hand. This is an argument that I develop in conversation with authors whose understandings of mediation (Nick Couldry and Sonia Livingstone), citizenship (Étienne Balibar), aesthetics (Jacques Rancière) and participation (Claire Bishop), among others, pay attention to issues of power dynamics.

My analysis will be structured into five steps: first, a description of *pUN*; second, a reflection on the idea of mediation as a connector between international affairs and contemporary art practices; third, a discussion of the project as an examination of the UN's rhetoric of democracy and deliberation; fourth, a reflection on the politics of representation of *pUN*, which inhabits the UN's foundational contradictions; fifth, concluding thoughts regarding the project's ability to foreground some of the UN's internal exclusions. As I will suggest, the art project stresses that the UN's rhetoric of democracy and deliberation is in tension with its modus operandi. However, rather than criticising the international organisation from an external position, *pUN* inhabited its contradictory symbols and rhetoric and used them as its subject, hence suggesting without prescribing the possibility of institutional reform. This said, the analysis will also emphasise the limits of the project to achieve what it implied, perhaps unintentionally—i.e. the possibility of UN reform—and hence the (partial) disjunction between the fields of art and international affairs.

Although the article's focus lies on an art project that engaged with the UN, its findings are potentially transferable to other international organisations—namely, to a reflection on the tensions between the viewership position that they demand and their openness (or lack therein) to regular forms of participation. Its conclusions also contribute to existing research on the overlaps between discussions of spectatorship and ongoing debates around citizenship. Indeed, the value of studying artworks that refer to official imagery and narratives for examining broader political and international questions will become clear throughout the article: artistic appropriation and dislocation can be understood as a type of feature-by-feature analysis, which compares and contrasts the

---

[2] For a summary of the origins and the history of the discipline, see Dikovitskaya (2005); for a discussion of the epistemological differences between visual culture and visual studies, see Moxey (2008).

[3] The project was subsequently displayed at the Hammer Museum in Los Angeles from 31 January to 24 May 2015. My analysis focuses on its first iteration.

institutional narratives of international organisations with their modes of work as well as art projects about such organisations. The ability to make explicit contradictions and blind spots in these subjects and surrounding discussions is the main strength of this approach.

Nonetheless, one must also acknowledge the main difficulty of studying this type of evidence: ascertaining whether there is a link between its scholarly analysis and the impact of the project, namely regarding how it was perceived by participants. While this would be an interesting focus for future research, I must stress that this relatively common critique of visual culture and art historical analysis derives from a mistaken conflation. This point confuses the fields' indebtedness to methods such as phenomenology and ethnography on the one hand, which allow them to take into consideration perception and embodied experience in their analyses of social phenomena, with the goal of the disciplines on the other hand: in the case of visual culture (the field with which I align this chapter), understanding the manifold meanings that images acquire as they emerge, circulate and change. This is made possible by the equal influence of other methods in the development of the discipline, such as semiotics and communication studies (Mitchell 1994, 2005). That is, although it would have been interesting to consider the response to *pUN*—in this case, how it was understood by its participants and viewers—, doing so isn't required to validate an analysis of the project inspired in visual culture scholarship. This differentiation is clear when one looks at *pUN*: whether participants and viewers saw it as a reflection on the UN's rhetoric (both textual and visual) or not does not change the fact that its participatory form enacted such a critique.

The People's United Nations (pUN)

Let us then consider the project in detail. As I will be arguing throughout the chapter, *pUN* foregrounded a set of fundamental contradictions of the UN.

Perusing several websites, databases and catalogues makes evident that the involvement of artists with the UN is only occasional and mostly indirect. Indeed, the number of artworks that can be found dealing explicitly with it is very low—which perhaps reflects the complexity of the organisation.[4] *PUN*, developed by the Mexican artist Pedro Reyes, is among the rare examples of an artistic engagement with this international organisation. It was presented at Performa 13, a biannual performance art festival staged in the Queens Museum, New York, and comprised an exhibition (on view from 9 November, 2013 to 30 March, 2014) and a performance (taking place at midday 23–24 November, 2013) (Reyes, 2013b). Reyes, born in 1972, lives and works in Mexico, and has participated in group exhibitions such as dOCUMENTA(13) in Kassel. He has risen to international

---

[4] For example, the visual culture scholar Gavin Grindon (2010) analyses the attempt by Copenhagen's cultural institutions to engage with the United Nations 2009 Climate Change Summit. Grindon concludes that it 'revealed another crisis in contemporary art's capacity to tackle issues of social change [...]. Instead, the art which most successfully engaged with the issues of climate change was that which had more affinity with extra-institutional activist practices' (Grindon 2010:10–11).

attention with projects such as *Palas por Pistolas* (Guns for Shovels) (2008), in which the artist took guns from the Mexican drugs war, melted them down and re-cast the metal as shovels. A prolific artist, Reyes has had solo exhibitions namely at Creative Time, New York, USA (2016); Dallas Contemporary, Texas, USA (2016); The Power Plant, Toronto, Canada (2014); Walker Art Center, Minneapolis, MN, USA (2011); Guggenheim Museum, New York, USA (2011) and his group exhibitions include The National Museum of XXI Century Arts (MAXXI), Rome (2015); Beijing Biennale, China (2014); dOCUMENTA (13), Kassel, Germany (2012); Liverpool Biennial, UK (2012); Gwangju Biennial, South Korea (2012) and the 50th Venice Biennale, Italy (2003).

The project originated from an invitation from Larissa Harris, curator of the Queens Museum, and marked the reopening of the building following extensive renovation. Two important facts about the museum informed the work. First, it had housed the UN General Assembly from 1946 to 1950 (before the move to the purpose-built UN headquarters). Second, the New York district of Queens, where the museum is situated, is one of the neighbourhoods in the world with the highest diversity per square mile. This led to the idea of developing two performances with a 193-member mock delegation comprising New York immigrants and their family members: all were either immigrants from the 195 members and observer states that currently make up the UN or had family connections to them. Under the official motto of the project—"hands-on with a vision" (see Figure 1)—the participants discussed issues ranging from gun controls to climate change. As is stated in the *pUN Workbook*:

> The seal of pUN is inspired by the hamsa (literally, "five" in Arabic). This open right hand with an eye at the center of the palm has been a symbol of protection across cultures and millennia. Originating in Africa, the hamsa predates Christianity and Islam. Workers' and peoples' movements have often been represented by a hand, sometimes holding a tool or closed in a fist. Here, the hand is open [...]. This benignant hand placed over an orb is meant to signal our mission to protect the planet. And here, its five fingers represent the world's five populated continents (Queens Museum. 2013b:3).

Drawing on a wide variety of conflict resolution techniques—including the Theatre of the Oppressed, a technique used for conflict resolution developed in the 1960s by Augusto Boal, a Brazilian stage-director; Force Field Analysis, a social science technique developed by Kurt Lewin; and techniques from couples therapy, to name but three—*pUN* sought alternative ways of confronting, discussing and resolving problems such as global poverty, food scarcity, drone attacks and weapons proliferation. Organised according to the structure of speed dating events, a bell rang to signal to the delegates that they should move to the next table and discuss a different subject. The programme of events included lectures by experts, which were followed by a vote from the delegates (see Figure 2). Provocatively, the project suggested that these techniques are potentially more productive than the deliberation methods employed by the UN, a forceful criticism of the effectiveness (or lack thereof) of traditional global diplomacy.

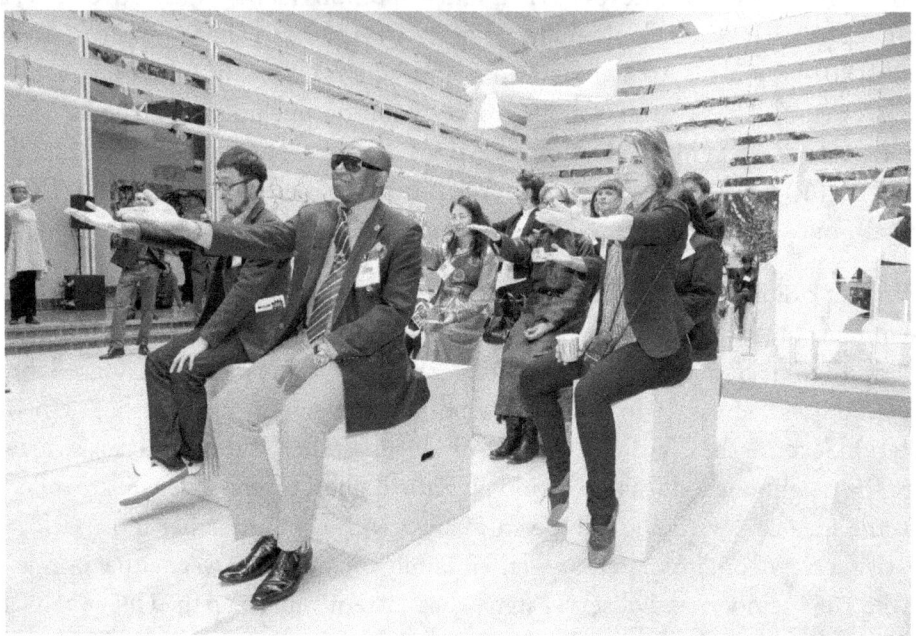

Figure 2: View of the performance. Courtesy Queens Museum, New York.

Mirroring what takes place in the UN's headquarters, museum visitors could experience the *pUN* activities through half-hour guided tours which included attendance of the sessions, the history of the UN and a tour of Reyes' exhibition inspired by the *pUN*'s underlying themes of dialogue and peace. *PUN also* overlapped with an event in which Peter Launsky-Tieffenthal, the then UN Under-Secretary-General for Communication and Public information, unveiled a plaque at the Museum with the following text engraved: "On this site, from 1946 to 1950, The United Nations General Assembly convened" (UN Blogs 2013). At this unveiling, Reyes presented Launsky-Tieffenthal with a petition from the General Assembly of *pUN* demanding arms disarmament on a global scale.

The *pUN* meetings and tours took place within an exhibition, which was composed of several sculptures created by Reyes for the atrium of the museum: namely, a miniature cityscape composed of seating cubes; the *Drone Dove*—merging the forms of a drone and a dove of peace (see Figures 2 and 3) and described as resembling

> both the United States Air Force Predator Drone, currently used for drone attacks, as well as the simple beauty of modern sculptures that depict doves in the postwar twentieth century, as seen in the work of Pablo Picasso and Isamu Noguchi. As a symbol, Drone Dove is a silent protest urging all governments to stop the use of unmanned vehicles in warfare (Reyes 2013a:266).

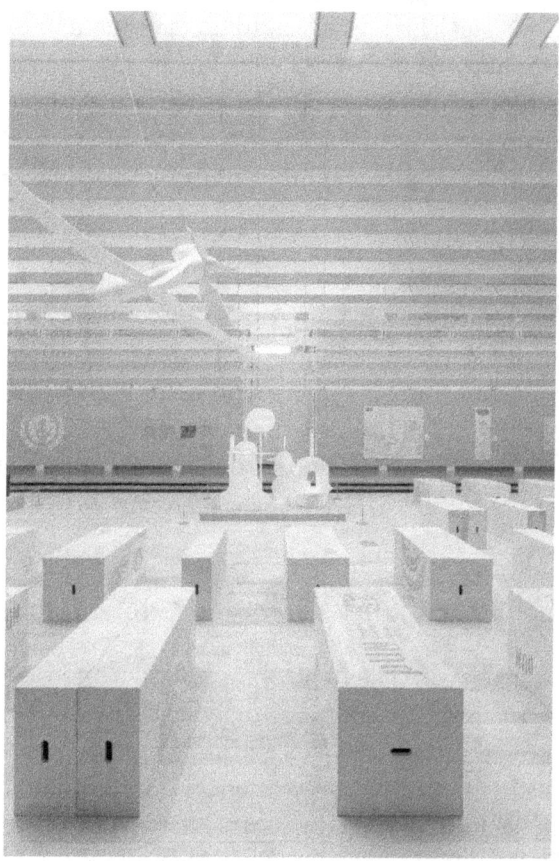

Figure 3: Exhibition view. Courtesy Queens Museum, New York

The atrium also included the *Colloquium*, a white sculpture of interlocking marble panels shaped like a blank cartoon speech-bubble; and *Disarm/Clock*, a weapon-clock made from gun parts which made a sound every quarter hour, which Reyes had made earlier in the context of the project *Disarm* (2012). These elements remained in the atrium of the museum until March 30, 2014. The sculptures were described on the website of the Queens Museum in the following way:

> with their frank embrace of symbolism, these sculptures provide a po-
> etic and inspiring backdrop for the *pUN* convening and representing its
> sincere optimism, serious and playful at once, to the Museum visitor
> after the event is over (Queens Museum 2013a).

However, by no means should this playfulness be seen as denying the seriousness of the issues discussed by the project. Rather, as the artist himself explained in an interview, "it is precisely the lighthearted spirit of play that allows the participants to engage in sub-jects whose magnitude would otherwise overwhelm us" (UN News Centre 2013). The difference between playing a game and the spirit of play was fundamental in this context. The performance (titled *pUN General Assembly*) functioned not as a self-contained game, in which only one participant can win to the detriment of his opponents, but as a playful platform. This allowed the participants to identify, even if provocatively, with the representatives of their nation state at the UN (taking the role of "citizen-delegates") as well as to speculate on the form that the institution would take if it served its mission without being influenced by politics and other constraints. As the artist stated,

> one of the main differences between *pUN* and the UN is that delegates at the UN represent their government. And governments have an agenda which is, first, their national interest; second, the interest of the [sic] their people; and third, the interest of the planet. In *pUN*, I think that the delegates are not concerned with representing their governments— they represent their nation-states, their people [...]. So they can take a stand with [sic] having a more global perspective. But I don't think *pUN* is in itself a critique of the UN. (Brooks and Reyes 2013)

Mediation: Linking International Affairs and Contemporary Art

I will discuss this idea (i.e. to what extent *pUN* can be understood as a critique of the UN) later in this article. Before doing so, I want to briefly reflect on the idea of visual mediation as a connector between international affairs and contemporary art that makes possible a focused reflection on the structuring consequences of mediating devices. Reyes' references to the UN took the form of visual references and tropes associated with the organisation, rather than direct references to specific deliberations, resolutions, treaty ratifications or to the UN's work on the ground. *pUN* can hence be understood as an artwork that is broadly aligned with discussions of visual mediation[5] and its role in legitimising the current geopolitical order. Indeed, as international relations scholars François Debrix and Cynthia Weber define it in *Rituals Of Mediation: International Politics And Social Meaning* (2003), mediation "is a site of representation, transformation, and pluralization where cultural and international rituals are performed. These rituals, in turn, perform what are taken to be culturals and internationals" (2003:vii). As we will see, by appropriating its images, *pUN* made the case that there are several breakages in the processes of mediation between the peoples in whose name the UN was founded, the functioning of the UN as an institution, its images, and the artistic appropriation of the latter.

---

[5] The concept of mediation (Roger Silverstone 2002, 2005) should not be confused with that of mediatisation. Nick Couldry discusses the differences between these two terms in detail in a piece that focuses on digital storytelling (2008, including their histories and definitions by key authors:4–9; see also Couldry and Hepp 2013). His argument is that mediatisation, in broad terms, refers to 'an essentially linear transformation from "pre-media" [...] to mediatized social states (2008:3) whilst mediation refers to the "heterogeneity of the transformations to which media give rise across a complex and divided social space rather than a single 'media logic' that is simultaneously transforming the whole of social space at once" (2008:3).

In doing so, *pUN* confirmed the relevance of Nick Couldry's questioning of the assumption of symmetry that is present in Roger Silverstone's definition of mediation. The latter author describes it as concerning "the fundamentally, but unevenly, dialectical process in which institutionalised media of communication [...], are involved in the general circulation of symbols in social life" (Silverstone 2002:762). However, Couldry finds Silverstone's definition "too friendly" (2008:8) towards the media. Rather, the former author also identifies

> two possibilities only hinted at in Silverstone's definition of mediation: first, that what we might call 'the space of media' is structured in important ways, durably and partly beyond the intervention of particular agents; and second that, because of that structuring, certain interactions, or 'dialectics'—between particular sites or agents—are closed off, isolating some pockets of mediation from the wider flow. (2008:8)

An interest in the specific ways, in which such a "closing off" takes place through the visual mediation of the UN, underlies the understanding of mediation that was in operation in my doctoral thesis[6], in which I discussed, namely, images of the UN such as its flag, photographs of its New York headquarters, the General Assembly and the Security Council as making the rhetorical argument regarding the continued relevance and legitimacy of the UN. That said, that is not the goal of this article. Rather, the next pages aim to demonstrate that the dialectical process that is identified by Silverstone can be activated—namely, through artistic appropriation.

In any case, two key discoveries of my analysis of the visual rhetoric of the UN are pertinent in the context of this article. First, the literature on aesthetics and the politics of representation often discusses the difficulty of representing violence and horror; rather, my analysis demonstrated that the attempt by the UN to visibly represent ideas such as peace, universality and inclusivity also remains unrealised. The institutional failure of the UN to fully enact such promises lied at the core of Reyes' project. Second, I discovered that the images of the UN perform rhetorically the change of threshold from the national to the international level as a focus of attention, debate and political action. In doing so, they contribute to legitimising the existence of the UN itself. It could be said that, paradoxically, *pUN* made a related case—not through scholarly analysis but by means of artistic appropriation and recombination. However, by asking participants to represent specific nation states in a performance based on the structure of the General Assembly, *pUN* also suggested the difficulty of fully enacting the movement from the national to the international unless the UN's structure is itself questioned.

The UN's Rhetoric of Democracy and Deliberation

Indeed, I will now argue that *pUN* can be seen as reflecting upon the tension between the rhetoric of deliberation and universality of the UN, its cosmopolitan values and as-

---

[6] I am currently transforming it into a monograph.

pirations, and its modus operandi—an argument that brings me to Étienne Balibar's discussion of equality.

The performance (titled, as I mentioned before, *pUN General Assembly*) referred to the modus operandi of the UN's General Assembly as its main inspiration, although the modular structure of the cubes in which the participants sat (which could be rearranged whenever necessary) also brought to mind the circular structure of the Security Council table. Before advancing, it is important to stress that the General Assembly's stated goal and priority is to reach either consensus or broad majorities. Each of its members (now 193, following the admission of Montenegro in 2006 and South Sudan in 2011) has one vote (article 18, 1) and important issues such as the election of members to councils[7] and recommendations concerning "international peace and security" can only be taken if a two-thirds majority of the members is involved (UN 1945, Article 18, 2). That is, its supranational focus is accompanied by a modus operandi organised around the historical model of the nation state—extending membership to preexisting political communities to which it accords equal formal power.

As for the central goal of the Security Council, that is the maintenance of peace and security—as is described in Chapter V of the Charter. In particular, points 1 and 2 of article 24 affirm that

1. In order to ensure prompt and effective action by the United Nations, its Members confer on the Security Council *primary responsibility for the maintenance of international peace and security* [...].

2. In discharging these duties the Security Council shall act *in accordance with the Purposes and Principles* of the United Nations (UN 1945 [original emphasis]).

However, the modus operandi of the Security Council is also in tension with these principles. The forum is composed of five permanent members (China, France, Russian Federation, United Kingdom and United States) and ten non-permanent members who are elected by the General Assembly for two-year terms. Each Council member has one vote and an affirmative vote of at least nine of the 15 members is needed to pass an action. Additionally, in the case of fundamental issues, nine votes, including the five of the permanent members holding veto power, are required for an action to proceed. This is particularly important since the Security Council has the power to establish peace enforcement operations, including international sanctions, and to authorise military action. Moreover, of all the organs of the UN, only the Council can take decisions that are enforceable under the Charter.

The flexibility of *pUN*'s seating cubes can be interpreted as highlighting the rigidity of the Council's membership structure (that is, its five permanent members, reproducing the geopolitical order of the post-war period). Additionally, the sculpture *Drone Dove*, com-

---

[7] For example, the Economic and Social Council, the Trusteeship Council and the Security Council (non-permanent members).

bining references to the UN's mission (to maintain and sustain understanding among different peoples) and to new and yet-to-be-regulated forms of warfare (the reference to the drone) suggested the shortcomings of the organisation to face emerging global challenges. Finally, I must mention the redesigned UN flag, which implicitly opposed the focus on the northern hemisphere of the official image. This is why, despite the artist's statement (mentioned earlier), it is difficult not to see Reyes' decision to combine traditional and experimental decision-making techniques as an indirect criticism of the UN. Indeed, the performance implicitly asked a question about the ideal form that the organisation would take if it were explicitly designed to fulfil its mission: building understanding and responding to global challenges in light of the long-term interests of the global population.

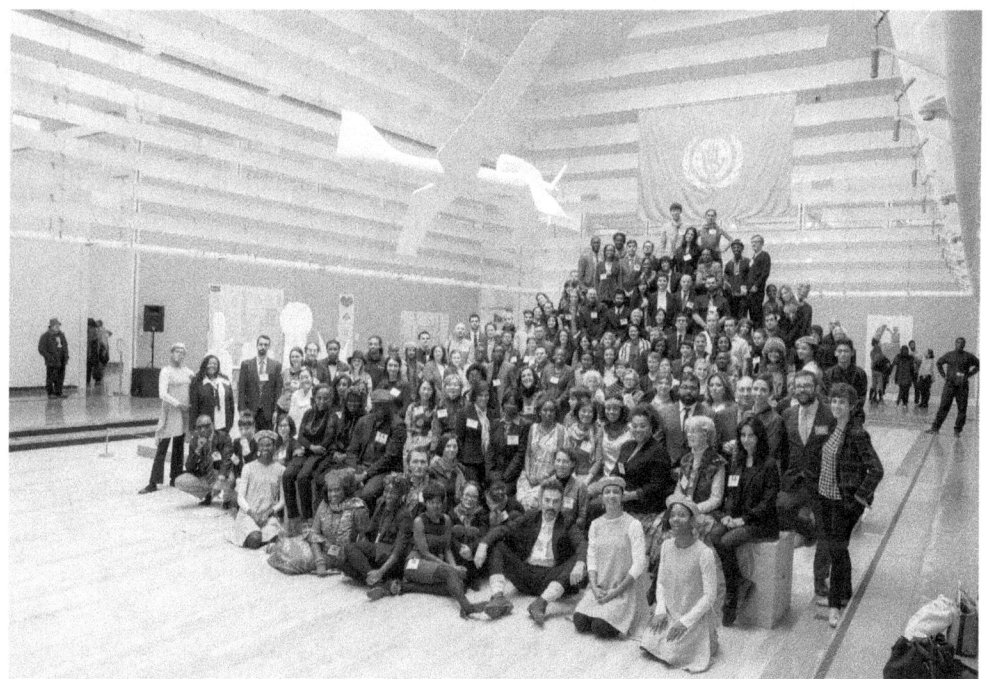

Figure 4: View of the performance. Courtesy Queens Museum, New York.

In this context, it is crucial to mention that the performance included individuals who, whether in representation of the countries from which they had immigrated or with family connections to the member state that they represented within *pUN*, lived in New York (see Figure 4). This suggests that some of them may have had American citizenship. In any case, the fact that most participants lived beyond the countries that they represented in the context of *pUN* demonstrated the insufficiency of the framework of the nation state to reflect mobility fluxes.

This tension leads me to an essay by philosopher Étienne Balibar (2016), in which he argues, influenced by Derrida, that the figure of the citizen is instituted in her naming as such. At the same time, the influence of Marxism in Balibar's work leads him to consider how this performative process is related to global power imbalances (most evident in the figure of the refugee). Discussing the difference between symbolic and formal equality in "A Hyperbolic Proposition" (2016), the author writes that "civic equality is indissociable from universality but separates it from community" (Balibar 2016). Indeed,

> either equality is "symbolic," which means that each individual, whatever his [sic] strengths, his power, and his property, is reputed to be equivalent to every individual in his capacity as citizen [...]. Or equality is "real," which means that citizenship will not exist unless the conditions of all individuals are equal. (Balibar 2016)

This highlights the existence of a problem within representative international politics, which not only is in tension with the idea of citizenship as a universal promise (as Balibar suggests) but also hasn't sufficiently expanded to reflect global changes in mobility and lifestyle (as *pUN* demonstrates). Additionally, and most crucially, this issue brings me to the tension between the UN's promise of equality and the separation of the global population according to political entities through which it acquires its rights. As the philosopher writes, "equality in fact cannot be limited [...]. In order to speak of "all citizens," it is necessary that somebody not be a citizen of said polity" (Balibar 2016). In light of Balibar's analysis, it becomes clear that, in exchange for being given a voice in *pUN*'s performance, the participants had to represent only one UN member state, which may have come at a symbolic cost to some of them—foregrounding as well the tension between the cosmopolitan values and aspirations of the UN and its modus operandi, which does not give permanent institutional representation to those who are refugees and stateless. Indeed, as is well known, the political ideal of cosmopolitanism (a form of belonging that does not assume the nation state as the bearer of rights and obligations) originated in Immanuel Kant's seminal essay "Perpetual Peace: A Philosophical Sketch" (1795). Among the several principles identified by Kant as necessary to achieve such global peace, the third definitive article states that "the law of world citizenship shall be limited to conditions of universal hospitality" (1795:105). The latter is here to be understood as the right of a stranger not to be treated as an enemy in a land that isn't her own. The nation-centric nature of the United Nations, which treats as equals states that welcome and respect the human rights of refugees and those that don't, reveals the organisation's limited enactment of this ideal.

Additionally, the opposition between the rigidity of the UN and the difficulty of accessing its fora on the one hand, and the open call for participants on the other hand, can be seen as highlighting the limits of the rhetorical claims of the UN—that is, the tension between its promise (to represent all individuals—"We, the People") and its structures (an organisation in which the member states are represented by individuals who are politically nominated, not elected—leading to debates that, like the blank speech-bubbles of the *Colloquium* sculpture, are not always characterised by the exchange of ideas). In doing so, the installation stressed the habitual position of the viewer vis-à-vis the UN: her lack of involvement.

The Politics of Representation

This leads me to the relation between *pUN*'s form and subject. I will argue that the combination of playfulness and shared action allowed the project to inhabit—rather than to criticise from a distant position—the UN's foundational antagonisms and exclusions.

As an exhibition and a participatory, cheerful practice that aimed to suggest, in a playful manner, alternative institutional and global possibilities, *pUN* was similar to the type of practices that are described by Nicolas Bourriaud in *Relational Aesthetics* (1998:13). However, central to the latter's argument is the idea that artists aim to elaborate meaning "collectively rather than in the privatised space of individual consumption" (Bishop 2005:116) as a way to respond to the Marxist critique of the reproduction of hegemonic ideology. That is, underlying Bourriaud's theory lies a belief in the emancipatory power of art as a site of (seemingly) equal, democratic relations. On the contrary, *pUN* did not share such an emancipatory intention. Rather, it aimed to playfully expand the political space (i.e. the debates that take place within the UN and its institutional framework—with which it experimented), which it did by stressing that which it usually excludes. This said, despite this fundamental difference, both Bourriaud and Reyes are united by their interest in nurturing the transition between the individual visitor and a shared symbolic space.

To better understand how this movement was at play in *pUN*, it is helpful to consider in more detail the significance of *pUN*'s appropriation of the emblem/flag of the UN. I will do so through a brief comparative discussion of the reception of Reyes' work and Dread Scott's *What is the Proper Way to Display a US Flag?* (1989). Doing so reveals that, although seemingly unremarkable, the absence of an overly negative reception to *pUN*'s appropriation of the UN flag is revealing of a crucial difference between its symbolic power and that of the flags of nation states. Scott's installation (1989) consisted of a shelf with an open book in which the visitors were invited to write, a montage of photographs of American flags draping the coffins of military personnel combined with protestors burning an American flag in response to the Vietnam War, and another flag in which the viewers could stand as they expressed their thoughts. Its reception was characterised by widespread criticism (see Scott, no date). The fact that the appropriation of one of the key symbols of the UN by Reyes was uncontested (to the best of my knowledge) is significant to an extent that cannot be explained by the difference between standing on or modifying a flag. Indeed, one can induce that a similar appropriation of the UN flag would have been unlikely to lead to the same level of criticism as Scott's. Conversely, one can imagine that an art piece based on a similar formal strategy to that of *pUN* but, rather, about the American democratic system would be the object of public debate. This analysis is confirmed by the widespread media coverage (Kennedy 2016; Rayner 2016) received by Reyes' subsequent project: *Doomocracy* (2016), an immersive installation in an abandoned terminal that asked viewers to reflect on the state of American politics. Altogether, this suggests the low-intensity symbolic (and affective) engagement of viewers with the UN and, conversely, the strong degree of attachment felt by many individuals vis-à-vis their nation states.

This said, the work of Jacques Rancière reveals that the two interventions have something else in common. Like Étienne Balibar, he was a student of Louis Althusser; this is reflected in Rancière's concern with equality. But while Balibar's work considers its fulfilment or lack thereof in light of who is defined as a citizen, Rancière develops an analogous analysis in aesthetics and pedagogy, among other fields. In this framework, and as is well known, Rancière's attempt to identify the fundamental modes of articulation between the political and the aesthetic in *The Politics of Aesthetics: The Distribution of the Sensible* (2000) leads him to conceive the distribution of the sensible as both the organisation of what can be said, seen, thought or heard, and as a distribution of images and places. In light of this statement, both Reyes' and Scott's interventions emerge as interested in expanding public conversations about the overlaps and disjunctions between the positions of the visitor of art museums, the citizen, the protester, the artist and, more broadly, of the politics of representation within the cultural and the political fields.

But there is another crucial dimension of *pUN* that is illuminated by Rancière's work: the position of the participant in Reyes' performance, which was aligned with the former's understanding of the spectator (evident both in his earlier work, such as in *The Ignorant Schoolmaster: Five Lessons in Intellectual Emancipation*, 1987, and in the argument developed in the well-known essay "The Emancipated Spectator" regarding the position of the spectator vis-à-vis the actor, 2009). The philosopher writes,

> we have not to turn spectators into actors. We have to acknowledge that any spectator already is an actor of his own story and that the actor also is the spectator of the same kind of story. We have not to turn the ignorant into learned persons, or, according to a mere scheme of overturn, make the student or the ignorant the master of his masters. (2009:279)

That is, the French author is critical of art practices that aim to emancipate their participants, which presupposes the ignorance of the latter. Rather, he proposes an aesthetics that isn't emancipatory (regarding, for example, the supposed domination of consumerism—an approach that Rancière sees as patronising) but, instead, offers viewers a possibility for active interpretation. This is why Rancière's model is characterised by the blurring of the boundaries between looking and doing (2009:102). Reyes' decision to place the participants (without whom there would be no performance) at the centre of his intervention highlights the similarity between his and Rancière's views on spectatorship. This is foregrounded in Reyes' description of the Theatre of the Oppressed as one of his main influences in *pUN Workbook* (2013).[8] As he states,

> theatre of the Oppressed stages situations that contain several social "errors." At a certain point the play stops and you—the spectator—are invited to become an actor, or a "spect-actor." [sic] [...] Rather than describing a new situation, the spect-actor [sic] acts it out. There are no experts here—knowledge that results from this experiment will be the best we can attain. (2013:10)

This "acting out the situation" is evident in the fact that *pUN's* events had no script— only broad guidelines such as their time, format and duration. That is, instead of being *about* the UN, the activities that composed the performance were joined by their echoing of the UN's mission and rhetoric: fostering and maintaining peace and understanding among peoples (hence *pUN's* focus on deliberation, relationship-building and the topics of the debates and other parts of the performance). This is why I see Reyes' approach as fundamentally analogous to that of the artist Mark Wallinger in *Oxymoron* (1996)—another rare explicit artistic engagement with political iconography. This artwork, a flag combining the design of the Union Jack with the colours of the Irish tricolour, was a reminder of the continued sectarianism in Northern Ireland. As the artist and scholar Dave Beech states in a review of the piece, the artwork was also an

> emblem of politicisation not because it takes on one of the sharpest political conflicts of our time, but because it internalises those antagonisms in its very fabric [...]. The first task of art's politicisation is to struggle for struggle. (Beech 2001)

That is, both artists engaged with political entities through their forms of visual (re)presentation, which they appropriated and combined. Additionally, like Beech suggests, both highlighted the inner divisions that characterise those institutions or countries yet are not usually visible in their official imagery—an absence that the artists corrected. In this view, and considering the piece's focus on the exclusionary character of citizenship (as I mentioned in relation to the work of Balibar), *pUN* can be seen as aligned with Laclau and Mouffe's radical understanding of democracy and the political (1985), which emphasises the centrality of conflict.

Finally, the significance of *pUN's* appropriation of the UN's images and narrative in this manner can be further understood if one considers the argument developed by Barbara Bolt. In *Art Beyond Representation: The Performative Power of the Image* (2004), and drawing on Heidegger's counter-representationalist idea of handling first developed in *Being and Time* (1927), the artist and scholar proposes that artistic practice exemplifies a relation of care that brings about a different understanding of the

---

[8] Which, I must note, mitigates the importance of emancipation as the original goal of these theatrical forms.

world to that offered by Cartesian representation. In this view, art and world are in a relationship of mutual indebtedness, in which the artist, the materials used by her and the creative process bring into appearance something that cannot be predicted fully by the artist. To make this case, Bold discusses Derrida's reading of Heidegger's work, which stresses the existence of movement within the latter (see "Sending: On Representation" 1982). As she writes, "the process of translation necessarily involves corruption. It is this corruption that produces permutations and brings about meta-morphosis" (2004:33–35).

To return to the initial part of my argument, Bolt's argument confirms that *pUN*'s highlighting of the coexistence of contradictory elements within the UN's rhetoric was made possible by its focus on mediation. That is, *pUN* not only used the UN as its topic; rather, it also considered the organisation's representation both in terms of how it represents itself and of who is represented in it. In doing so, *pUN* foregrounded the political dimension (understood in light of Rancière's work, that is, as a distribution of words and images, and hence of the sayable and the imaginable, 2000) of representation within and of an international organisation that presents itself as universal and inclusive. In this context, the performative aspect of the piece was crucial. As Reyes affirmed:

> The performative aspect starts with the presence of one person from every country on Earth. [...]. But it's important that these activities ac-tually *happen*. [...]. It's very playful, but very serious, and that's the kind of ambiguity we want. And that's precisely why it's called pUN. You have these two ideas to interpret. A thin line between being serious and doing pranks. (Brooks and Reyes 2013)

That is, appropriating and performing the UN's imagery and rhetoric, the artwork made visible the tension between the mission, values and ideas (such as universality) based on which the UN is discursively founded, and its modus operandi, which is exclusionary. *pUN*'s gesture can hence be understood as one not of critique but of criticality (Rogoff 2003) in that, instead of criticising the UN from an external position, it inhabited its contradictory symbols and rhetoric and used them as its subject, hence suggesting with-out prescribing the possibility of institutional reform (echoing similar calls for reform by UN experts, e.g. Slaughter 2005; Weiss and Thakur 2010).

Conclusion: Foregrounding the Instability Within the UN

Finally, the artwork revealed the impotence of the artistic realm—the latter can crit-icise the political sphere (here understood in a strict sense) but it cannot enact such ideas. This said, artistic forms of engagement with political debates may influence public discourse—by creating spaces for discussion and by considering issues that tend to be overlooked.

This becomes clear when one considers Sonia Livingstone's work, which focuses namely on the relation between mediation and the possibility of political action. In "On the relation between audiences and publics" (2005), the media scholar argues that "we need an account of the formation of public opinion and of citizens—early expressions of interest, exploration of experience, tentative trying out of viewpoints" (Livingstone 2005:29). She suggests developing such an account by focusing on the realm of the civic, which is required by political action without, however, necessarily leading to the latter. This is key in the case of *pUN*—an artistic engagement with an international organisation that isn't open to regular forms of participation from the global citizens in whose name it speaks. The author also argues that paying attention to the civic demands an expanded understanding of citizenship—one that includes those moments in which one is confused and unsure of where one stands on specific political issues, i.e. "a domain of pre-political consideration, of unease with states of being, rather than as a monument to specific rights, duties or identities" (Hermes and Stello 2000:219 cited in Livingstone 2005:35). As such, this understanding of citizenship is also accompanied by a redefinition of the notion of public as "an ongoing space of encounter for discourse [...], a context of interaction" (2005:62). I see *pUN* as exemplifying the potential of art practices to embody such spaces of civic interaction and pre-political encounters.

In doing so, the intervention avoided the erroneous conflation of dialogue and equality that art historian and critic Claire Bishop identifies at being at play, for example, in the work of Rirkrit Tiravanija, in which "relations of conflict are erased rather than sustained" (2005:119). This is particularly evident when *pUN* suggested the limited enactment of the Habermasian discourse theory of deliberative democracy (1984, 1992) within the UN's General Assembly. Additionally, *pUN* stressed the difference between the People (referring to the category through which one becomes a citizen and acquires rights) on the one hand, and the more mobile experience of western populations (and hence viewers) on the other. Indeed, as I mentioned earlier, the participants in *pUN*'s performance lived in New York, but they didn't necessarily share a history or political identity.

This is why I see *pUN* as exemplifying the two ways how, according to Grant Kester, dialogical art practices are able to "[retain the] power of aesthetic dialogue without recourse to a universalising philosophical framework" (2004:14) such as that of Habermas. On the one hand, Kester writes, they reject claims of universality. That is, such practices are

> based on the generation of a local consensual knowledge that is only provisionally binding [...]. It is possible to engage in communicative interaction across boundaries of difference without the legitimating framework of a universal discursive system because the necessary framework is established through the interaction itself. (Kester 2004:112)

Second, the art historian writes, dialogical practices assume that "subjectivity is formed *through* discourse and intersubjective exchange itself. Discourse [...] is itself intended to model subjectivity" (Kester 2004:112). This idea (of discourse as key in avoiding the assumption and the reinforcement of preexisting identities) leads me to *pUN's own* modelling of alternative modes of problem-solving within the UN—which it does, however, without questioning the centrality of the nation state as the institution's organising principle.

It is helpful to briefly return to the work of Jacques Derrida to clarify the significance of this point. As is well known, Derrida argues that both representation and meaning emerge through *différance*, a process of continuous reinscription and alteration. Specifically, in "The Parergon" (1978), the French philosopher engages with a painting by Van Gogh, questioning the assumption developed by Kant in *Critique of Judgment* (1790) regarding the existence of an *a priori* essence of beauty. Particularly important for the analysis of *pUN* is Derrida's examination of a footnote in the third *Critique*—in which Kant defines the "parerga" as that which lies outside the artistic work. While Kant defines it as an "ornament", i.e. as a supplement to the "ergon" (the work), Derrida discusses the term as a "frame" or "edge" (Derrida 1978), i.e. as a supplement that is both outside and inside the work itself. In short, Derrida concludes that there is always an excess of meaning within any representational attempt. In this view, painting (as well as arguably all other artistic mediums) emerges as a manifestation of the notion of iterability or repetition with a difference.

I see Reyes' intervention as not only appropriating such an excess, but as also doing so in a way that stressed that which the images and the official rhetoric of the UN reject: its lack of internal coherence, its exclusions, the tension between its cosmopolitan aspirations and the crucial role of the nation state within it. To put it clearly, the UN's edge (to use Derrida's term) is, in fact, internal to the organisation. This is why it is so significant that *pUN* didn't reject the important role of the nation state within the UN's modus operandi—rather, it foregrounded it as a process of exclusion.

To conclude, it is precisely because it placed at its centre the instability of the images and the rhetoric of the UN in an anti-exclusionary gesture that the artwork was able to suggest a conversation regarding its mission and modus operandi. That is, the intervention did more than simply manifesting the complexity of the rhetoric of the UN, which it appropriated or to which it referred. Rather, by inhabiting such a rhetoric, Reyes highlighted its exclusions and, consequently, the potentially dialectical character of mediation that, as I mentioned in the beginning of this article, is identified—albeit in different ways—by both Silverstone (2002) and Couldry (2008). In doing so, the project foregrounded possible forms of—not emancipated, but, rather—*activated* viewership vis-à-vis the UN.

At the same time, although *pUN* aimed to interrupt the model of involvement without interference of the viewers regarding the UN, its examination made evident the project's inability to deliver the logical consequence of what it suggests: the need for institutional reform of the UN. And yet, paradoxically, *pUN's* own impotence may have been one of its strongest characteristics as an artistic intervention. Despite suggesting the transition from the realm of individual spectatorship of the UN to that of collective action with political and institutional impact, *pUN's* simultaneously semi-serious and semi-playful stance highlighted that such action can only happen when the visitor leaves the museum and begins to organise. By implicitly acknowledging the limits of the art world, *pUN* stressed the autonomy and the power of the visitor to achieve, as a citizen, what art can only suggest or demand.

References

Balibar, Étienne. (2016) *A Hyperbolic Proposition.* <http://www.e-flux.com/journal/78/82724/a-hyperbolic-proposition> (Accessed 17 December 2016).

Beech, Dave. (2001) *Art For All? (Administrator 2 Administrator).* <http://www.metamute.org/editorial/articles/art-all-administrator-2-administrator> (Accessed 10 February 2017).

Bishop, Claire. (2005) *Installation Art: A Critical History.* London: Tate Publishing.

Bolt, Barbara. (2004) *Art Beyond Representation: The Performative Power of the Image.* London: I. B. Tauris.

Bourriaud, Nicholas. (2002 [1998]) *Relational Aesthetics,* trans. Simon Pleasance and Fronza Woods. Paris: Les Presses du Réel.

Brooks, Katherine, and Pedro Reyes. (2013) *Pedro Reyes is Solving the World's problems, One Art Performance at a Time.* <http://www.huffingtonpost.com/2013/11/11/pedro-reyes_n_4242275.html> (Accessed 12 August 2014).

Carles, Nathalie Rivère de Carles. (2016) *Early Modern Diplomacy, Theatre and Soft Power: The Making of Peace.* London: Palgrave Macmillan.

Clements, Paul. (2016) *The Creative Underground: Art, Politics and Everyday Life.* London: Taylor & Francis.

Couldry, Nick. (2008) Digital Storytelling, Media Research and Democracy: Conceptual Choices and Alternative Futures. In *Digital Storytelling, Mediatized Stories: Self-representations in New Media,* ed. Knut Lundby, 41–60. New York: Peter Lang Publishing.

Couldry, Nick, and Andreas Hepp. (2013) Conceptualising mediatization: Contexts, traditions, arguments. *Communication Theory* 23 (3): 191–202.

Dâmaso, Mafalda. (2017) *Unstable Mediation – Regarding the United Nations as a Visual Entity.* Doctoral thesis.

Debrix, François, and Cynthia Weber. (eds). (2003) *Rituals of Mediation: International Politics And Social Meaning.* Minneapolis: University of Minnesota Press.

Derrida, Jacques. (1988 [1972]) Signature Event Context. In *Limited Inc,* ed. Gerald Graff, 1–24. Evanston, IL: Northwestern University Press.

Derrida, Jacques. (1987 [1978]) The Parergon. In *The Truth in Painting,* trans. Geoff Bennington and Ian McLeod, 17–147. Chicago: The University of Chicago Press.

Dikovitskaya, Margarita. (2005) *Visual Culture: The Study of the Visual After the Cultural Turn.* Cambridge, MA: MIT Press.

Frascina, Francis. (1999) *Art, Politics and Dissent: Aspects of the Art Left in Sixties America.* Manchester: Manchester University Press.

Gielen, Pascal. (2015) *The Murmuring of the Artistic Multitude: Global Art, Politics and Post-Fordism.* Amsterdam: Valiz.

Grindon, Gavin. (2010) Art, Activism and Climate Change. *Art Monthly* 333: 9–12.

Golan, Romy. (1995) *Modernity and Nostalgia: Art and Politics in France Between the Wars.* New Haven: Yale University Press.

Habermas, Jürgen. (1997 [1984]) *The Theory of Communicative Action: Reason and the Rationalization of Society.* (vol.1), trans. Thomas McCarthy. Cambridge, UK: Polity Press.

Habermas, Jürgen. (1996 [1992]) *Between Facts and Norms: Contributions to a Discourse Theory of Law and Democracy,* trans. William Rehg. Cambridge, MA: MIT Press.

Hampel, Annika. (2017) *Fair Cooperation: A New Paradigm for Cultural Diplomacy and Arts Management.* Brussels: ENCATC.

Harper, Dennis. (ed.) (2012) *Art Interrupted: Advancing American Art and the Politics of Cultural Diplomacy.* Athens: Georgia Museum of Art.

Harris, Jonathan. (2007) *Value, Art, Politics: Criticism, Meaning and Interpretation After Postmodernism.* Liverpool: Liverpool University Press.

Hjarvard, Stig. (2004) From bricks to bytes: The Mediatization of a Global Toy Industry. In *European Culture and the Media,* ed. Ib Bondebjerg and Peter Golding, 43–63. Bristol: Intellect Ltd.

Heidegger, Martin. (1996 [1927]) *Being and Time,* trans. Joan Stambauch. New York: State University of New York Press.

Kane, Patrick. (2013) *The Politics of Art in Modern Egypt: Aesthetics, Ideology and Na-*

tion-Building. London: I.B.Tauris.

Kant, Immanuel. (1914 [1790]). *Critique of Judgement,* trans. John Bernard. London: Macmillan.

Kant, Immanuel. (1991 [1795]) Perpetual Peace: A Philosophical Sketch. In *Kant: Political Writings,* ed. Hans Reiss, trans. H. B. Lisbet. 93–130. Cambridge: Cambridge University Press.

Kennedy, Randy. (2016) *'Doomocracy' Puts the Politics of Fear on Display in Brooklyn.* <https://www.nytimes.com/2016/10/07/arts/design/doomocracy-pedro-reyes-brooklyn-army-terminal.html> (Accessed 5 March 2017).

Kester, Grant. (2004) *Conversation Pieces: Community and Communication in Modern Art.* Berkeley, CA: University of California Press.

Kidd, Dustin. (2014) *Legislating Creativity: The Intersections of Art and Politics.* London: Routledge.

Laclau, Ernesto, and Chantal Mouffe. (2014 [1985]) *Hegemony and Socialist Strategy: Toward a Radical Democratic Politics.* London: Verso.

Livingstone, Sonia. (2005) On the Relation Between Audiences and Publics. In *Audiences and Publics: When Cultural Engagement Matters for the Public Sphere,* ed. Sonia Livingstone, 17–41. Bristol, UK: Intellect Books.

Lobel, Michael. (2009) *James Rosenquist: Pop Art, Politics, and History in the 1960s.* Berkeley, CA: University of California Press.

Lord, Gail, and Ngaire Blankenberg. (eds). (2015) *Cities, Museums and Soft Power.* Lanham, MA: Rowman & Littlefield.

Mikkonen, Simo, and Pekka Suutari. (eds). (2015) *Music, Art and Diplomacy: East-West Cultural Interactions and the Cold War.* London: Routledge.

Mitchell, W.J.T. (1994) *Picture Theory: Essays on Verbal and Visual Representation.* Chicago, IL: University of Chicago Press.

Mitchell, W.J.T. (2005) *What Do Pictures Want?: The Lives and Loves of Images.* Chicago, IL: University of Chicago Press.

Moxey, Keith. (2008) Visual Studies and the Iconic Turn. *Journal of Visual Culture* 7: 131–146.

Nisbett, Melissa. (2016) Who Holds the Power in Soft Power?. *Arts & International Affairs.* <http://theartsjournal.net/2016/03/13/nisbett/> (Accessed 5 August 2017).

Pearson, Christopher. (2017) *Designing UNESCO: Art, Architecture and International Politics at Mid-Century.* London: Routledge.

Queens Museum. (2013a) Pedro Reyes's: The people's United Nations (pUN). <http://www.queensmuseum.org/exhibitions/2013/11/09/pedro-reyes-the-peoples-united-nations-pun-2/> (Accessed 27 July 2017).

Queens Museum. (2013b) *pUN Workbook.* New York: Queens Museum.

Rancière, Jacques. (1991 [1987]) *The Ignorant Schoolmaster: Five Lessons in Intellectual Emancipation,* trans. Kristin Ross. Stanford, CA: Stanford University Press.

Rancière, Jacques. (2004 [2000]) *The Politics of Aesthetics: The Distribution of the Sensible,* trans. Gabriel Rockhill. London: Continuum.

Rayner, Alex. (2016) *Doomocracy: The Funhouse Haunted by Trump and Clinton.* <https://www.theguardian.com/artanddesign/2016/sep/22/doomocracy-art-installation-pedro-reyes-haunted-trump-and-clinton> (Accessed 5 May 2017).

Reyes, Pedro. (2013a) *ad usum: to be used.* ed. José Luis Falconi. Cambridge, MA: Harvard University Press.

Reyes, Pedro. (2013b) People's United Nations (pUN). <http://www.pedroreyes.net/pun.php?szLang=en&Area=work> (Accessed 27 August 2017).

Rogoff, Irit. (2003) *From Criticism to Critique to Criticality.* <http://eipcp.net/transversal/0806/rogoff1/en> (Accessed 27 July 2017).

Scott, Dread. (no date) *What is the Proper Way to Display a US Flag?.* <http://www.dreadscott.net/works/what-is-the-properway-to-display-a-us-flag/> (Accessed 1 March 2017).

Schulz, Winfried. (2004) Reconstructing Mediatization as an Analytical Concept. *European Journal of Communication* 19 (1): 87–101.

Selz, Peter, and Susan Landauer. (2006) *Art of Engagement: Visual Politics in California and Beyond.* Berkeley, CA: University of California Press.

Silverstone, Roger. (2002) Complicity and Collusion in the Mediation of Everyday Life. *New Literary History* 33 (4): 761–780.

Silverstone, Roger. (2005) The Sociology of Mediation and Communication. In *The Sage Handbook of Sociology,* eds. Craig Calhoun, Chris Rojek, and Bryan Turner, 188–207. London: SAGE Publications.

Slaughter, Anne-Marie. (2005) Reform: Security, Solidarity, and Sovereignty: The Grand Themes of UN Reform. *The American Journal of International Law* 99 (3): 619–631.

UN. (1945) *Charter of the United Nations and Statute of the International Court of Justice.* <http://www.un.org/en/charter-united-nations/index.html>. (Accessed 28 August 2017).

UN Blogs. (2013) *The People's United Nations (pUN) Exhibition at the Queens Museum.* <http://blogs.un.orgblog/2013/11/26/the-peoples-united-nations-pun-exhibition-at-the-queens-museum/#sthash.YJQ5hBUS.dpbs> (Accessed 10 July 2014).

UN News Centre. (2013) *Inspired by United Nations, New York Museum takes Unique Look at Tackling Global Challenges.* <http://www.un.org/apps/news/story.asp?News ID=46585#.U6h8s6iLZ1k.> (Accessed 15 June 2014).

Weiss, Thomas, and Ramesh Thakur. (2010) *Global Governance and the UN: An Unfinished Journey.* Bloomington: Indiana University Press.

Watanabe, Yasuhi, and David McConnell. (2008) *Soft Power Superpowers: Cultural and National Assets of Japan and the United States.* London: Routledge.

GOODBYE TO THE NATIONAL ENDOWMENT FOR THE ARTS?

NAOMI ADIV

Portland State University

Naomi Adiv is Assistant Professor of Urban Studies and Planning at Portland State University. She holds a PhD in Geography from the CUNY Graduate Center (New York City), and a Master's degree in Community Development at UC-Davis, with a focus on Community Arts.

In the shadow of the truly egregious policies rolled out by the Trump administration in their first year in office (anti-Muslim and anti-immigrant policies, de-staffing the State Department into paralysis, shrinking national monuments, strangling the ACA), and a general tone of chaos surrounding the office of the presidency, a standing threat remains. That is: among other cuts, freezes and gag orders, the administration has vowed to de-fund the National Endowment for the Arts (NEA), National Endowment for the Humanities (NEH) and the Corporation for Public Broadcasting (CPB). Here, I demonstrate how current political arguments around defunding the NEA are derived from a larger political model of dismantling the state apparatus, and purposely conflate fiscal and symbolic rationales in an attempt to influence cultural policy.

When the plan for cutting federal funding for culture was first announced, defenders of the NEA, NEH and CPB moved quickly, asking concerned Americans to sign this petition, call that office, and so forth. Those who are actively fighting the cuts note how the arts and humanities programs that are supported by these agencies enrich the lives of everyday Americans in rural and urban areas of all fifty states. Furthermore, defenders explain, myriad cultural stalwarts—from public libraries to local orchestras to public radio—are attached to these workhorse agencies, which themselves operate on shoestring budgets. Lately, the smallness of the NEA budget is taken as a unit of currency, as in: *this* [bomber, bureaucratic measure, security detail] *is three times the NEA's whole annual budget.*

Fairly often, the appeal—*stop cuts to arts and culture!*—includes a graph or pie chart, demonstrating that the NEA receives an infinitesimal percentage of the Federal Budget. The National Assembly of State Arts Agencies (NASAA) reports:

> The $146 million budget of the National Endowment for the Arts (NEA) represents just 0.012% (about one one-hundredth of one percent) of federal discretionary spending. The NEA has sustained signif-

icant budget reductions. NEA appropriations have declined by $21.5 million (−13%) in the last three federal budgets.

The NASAA goes on to explain that even these meager funds create jobs, stimulate local economies and improve education. Put in these terms, the general argument is that if Americans only knew how valuable these organizations are—and how far-reaching—especially compared to the much bigger wastrels (i.e. Department of Defense or, in recent days, the president's vacation spending), we would all be up in arms and we would have the good sense to join together to preserve them.

Others insist that the cuts are just a political proxy, such as in the case of CultureGRRL (Lee Rosenbaum) at ArtsJournal, who writes:

> Unfortunately, whenever there's a call to prune the budget, the NEA and NEH are low-hanging fruit. They're worth more for their symbolic value—an expendable expense when politicians want to appear fiscally frugal—than they worth are [sic] for their negligible impact on the government's gargantuan outlays.

And while I do not disagree with this sentiment, "symbolic value"—that is, symbolizing fiscal prudence—is not, in fact, the only logic under which these cuts are being made.

Indeed, in launching a defense of the NEA (and like organizations) that extols its efficacy as an economic engine, albeit one with deep cultural value, its defenders may be missing an opportunity to directly contest the arguments that the right is making about the NEA. The NEA's opponents are not simply arguing that the dollars we spend are a bad spending choice; rather, they are revitalizing old culture war tropes, and then hiding behind absolutist claims about limited government. Thus, as artists, academics and community-level cultural workers rush to save these small organizational and funding homes—and, by proxy, their merit on the national stage—we should also consider how we arrived at the current assault.

When the NEA was founded in 1965 under the Johnson administration,[1] with a budget of 2.4 million, the legislation that brought it (and the accompanying National Endowment for the Humanities) into existence stated:

> ... the practice of art and the study of humanities requires constant dedication and devotion and that, while no government can call a great artist or scholar into existence, it is necessary and appropriate for the federal government to help create and sustain not only a climate encouraging freedom of thought, imagination and inquiry, but also the material conditions facilitating the release of this creative talent.

---

[1] This process was initiated by President Kennedy, whose Executive Order 11112 established the President's Advisory Council on the Arts in 1963 (Koostra/NEA 2000).

As an additional part of the charter, the NEA was set up with peer review panels of re-spected artists to choose grants, "buffering grants from political oversight and empha-sizing artistic freedom over democratic accountability" (Lewis and Brooks 2005:9). Monies appropriated by congress to funding the NEA increased throughout the 1960s and 1970s—largely under the leadership of Nancy Hanks—with its projects gaining in scope and prestige.

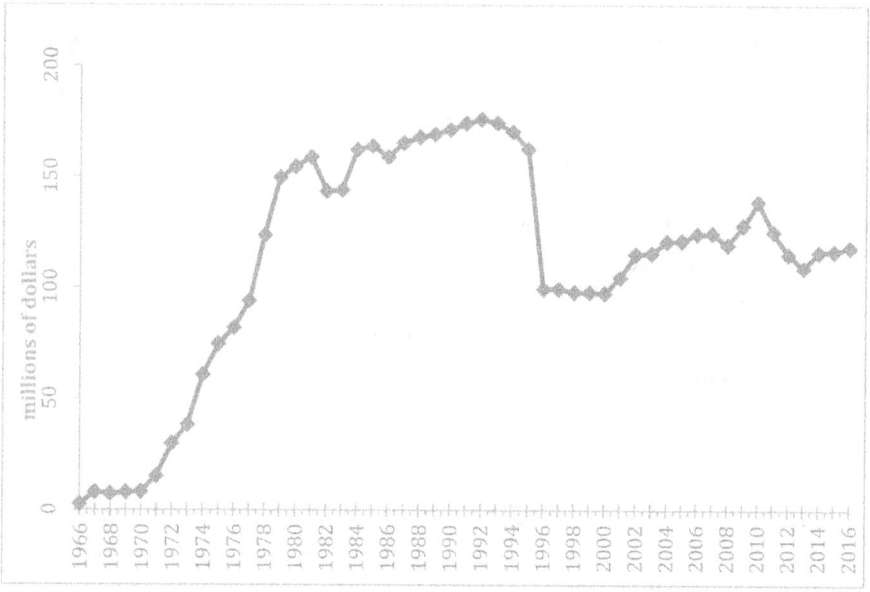

Figure 1: NEA funding 1966–2016. Source: NEA Annual Reports
https://www.arts.gov/about/annual-reports

NEA funding climbed for two decades until falling off steeply twice: the first time in 1982 during the Reagan administration, and the second in 1996, under the Clinton adminis-tration in the context of what would come to be known as the "Culture Wars" (Bolton 1992). At these junctures, the conservative legislative project of *making* NEA funding political took off by declaring arts having to do with gender and sexuality "obscene," or by rehearsing class-based arguments about the snobbery of cultural organizations. Since that time, agency funding has more or less flatlined (with a small bump in 2010 under Obama's economic stimulus bill), with its annual budget hovering around $120 million for the last decade or so.

Examining the 2017 CATO Handbook for Policymakers (which has its earliest edition on the website from 1995) under the subheading "Cutting Federal Departments and Programs," one finds Chapter #53: Cultural Agencies. At the top of the page is the lan-guage we plainly see in the Trump agenda:

Congress should

- eliminate the National Endowment for the Arts,
- eliminate the National Endowment for the Humanities, and
- defund the Corporation for Public Broadcasting

Finding a document that so nakedly lays out this policy serves as a reminder that many of the seemingly abrupt plans of the current administration (and its allies in Congress) execute a project that has been developed over decades of accusing the progressive wing of American politics—particularly in the realm of arts and culture—of elitism and the exclusion of "everyday" people. A great deal of energy has gone into building up popular support for this message, until such time as policies could be rolled out by the most conservative elements of the Republican party.[2] The result is cultural policy—or elimination thereof—based in political ideology.

The mechanism for this process requires a powerful sleight of hand between material and symbolic claims about government spending. As CultureGRRL points out regarding "symbolic value," cutting the NEA or NEH is a *performance* of fiscal responsibility, as opposed to the actual thing. Yet, the symbolic and the material are not entirely discernable, especially when the budgets are in the hundreds of millions of dollars (a large-sounding sum to regular Americans), and have real effects—a fact of which both sides are acutely aware.

Important to note is that the CATO document is not unique in its approach, but is a good example of the rationale for dismantling state cultural agencies. In order to do so, the authors take a few different tacks in the space of a relatively short document. These fall broadly into the categories of (1) government overreach, (2) protecting the purity of arts and culture, and (3) class-based arguments.

In the first category, the authors invoke the legal powers afforded to government through their interpretation of the Constitution:

> In a society that constitutionally limits the powers of government and maximizes individual liberty, there is no justification for the forcible transfer of money from taxpayers to artists, scholars, and broadcasters. (535)

Of course, the government transfers wealth from taxpayers to many kinds of actors all the time through appropriations, tax cuts, subsidies, etc., but this is a way for the authors to link up this particular policy prescription with a whole host of other market-based notions about how to distribute resources (for health care, education, etc.), which they do throughout the rest of the handbook.

---

[2] In the nine-page document that follows, the terms for cutting these institutions are laid out, and connected to the political philosophy of the CATO Institute, a libertarian think tank that has operated since 1977, providing federal and other lawmakers with their policy prescriptions in areas ranging from health care to foreign policy.

This sets us up for the second category—arts as ideologically pure—in which the rhetorical game is two-pronged. In both cases, we are pushed to understand the small number of dollars spent as material *and* symbolic. First:

> Note that the amount of arts funding in the federal budget is quite small. That might be taken as a defense of the funding, were it not for the important reasons to avoid any government funding of something as intimate yet powerful as artistic expression. (536)

The number is admittedly small, but—the authors say—we make this claim because art *is* important, not because it *isn't.*

The second prong of the ideological purity argument speaks more to conservative *values.* In order to do this, the authors remind us of controversial NEA-funded works, harkening back to the culture wars of the mid-1990s when the conservative "Contract with America" congress most effectively slashed the NEA budget:

> Among its more famous and controversial grant recipients were artist Andres Serrano, whose exhibit featured a photograph of a plastic crucifix in a jar of his own urine, and the Institute of Contemporary Art in Philadelphia, which sponsored a traveling exhibition of the late Robert Mapplethorpe's homoerotic photographs. (535)[3]

That tap on the shoulder about controversial art is not because we cannot take it, assert the authors; on the contrary, this is important stuff and therefore the government should keep its grubby paws away. (Worth noting here is that this section has not been updated very much in this edition, so trotting out these now-25-year-old examples is either still wildly relevant to their readership, or the best example they can come up with.)

In the third group—class-based arguments—the authors assert that federal arts and culture funds provide a subsidy for elite entertainment:

> Since art museums, symphony orchestras, humanities scholarship, and public television and radio are enjoyed predominantly by people of greater-than-average income and education, the federal cultural agencies oversee a fundamentally unfair transfer of wealth from the lower classes up .... (537)

In this rhetoric, government support of culture benefits an elite class that robs from the poor to entertain the rich. Another version of this, which one can find throughout the

---

[3] This sentiment is repeated again in the conclusion to this section:

> Because art is so powerful, because it deals with such basic human truths, we dare not entangle it with coercive government power. That means no censorship or regulation of art. It also means no tax-funded subsidies for arts and artists, for when government gets into the arts funding business, we get political conflicts. (541)

literature on de-funding federal cultural agencies goes, *the arts should be subject to market forces! Why do some people get to choose the symphony/ballet/museum for the rest of us?* Once again, the material and the symbolic are conflated to the point where they become difficult to disentangle. It *is* true that some kinds of entertainment (classical music, sculpture) receive federal dollars, while others (action movies, NASCAR) do not.

It is here that the NASAA argument (above)—which demonstrates that federal arts funding is distributed widely across American communities—makes the most sense. Local agencies of arts and culture require ongoing local maintenance, and ongoing reliable funding to make sure that someone is able to mind the store. The NEA makes art happen for all kinds of people in all kinds of places, even those without wealthy local foundations or edgy art scenes.

No matter. In the last moment, the CATO authors circle back around, claiming that their previous points were actually *not* their previous points even though they brought them up in the first place.

> No, the issue is neither the content of the work subsidized nor the expense. Taxpayer subsidy of the arts, scholarship, and broadcasting is inappropriate because it is outside the range of the proper functions of government, and as such it needlessly politicizes, and therefore corrupts, an area of life that should be left untainted by politics. (539)

It is a clever rationale, but not in fact the argument that the authors have been making throughout the rest of the document. Rather, they have busily set about attacking the actual workings of cultural agencies, only to repudiate those claims as a supposed matter of principle.

Alongside the material question of how our tax dollars should be spent, two kinds of symbolism operate. One is budget reduction as a symbol of fiscal responsibility; the other is art as a symbol of social permissiveness. Opponents of the NEA conflate these on purpose, and to great effect.

What ought the response be? The NEA (and other cultural agencies) are not *good* because they run on next-to-nothing; indeed, their budgets should be increased so they can run effectively and so more kinds of people can make—and be exposed to—more kinds of art. Progressive supporters of art need to step away from culture war tropes, and not get hauled into a media spin cycle of arguments with people howling about photographs Robert Mapplethorpe made in the early 1990s. The NEA, though not without its flaws, is dedicated to making art flourish in American communities of all kinds, and this is most consequential at this moment when creative expression has a mark on its back.

Like so much of the authoritarian policy agenda of the Trump administration, a detailed, long-standing plan and a pointed architecture lurk behind the policies, a set of tactics based in an overarching strategy to consolidate power and wealth in the hands of a very few as they tell very many that the terms of debate are, in fact, about a clash of values. Defunding our cultural agencies has diminished—and will continue to diminish—the nation's entryways to everyday democratic practice in ways both symbolic and material.

References

Bolton, Richard (ed.). (1992) *Culture Wars: Documents from the Recent Controversies in the Arts*. New York: The New Press.

CATO Handbook for Policy Makers. (2017) 8th Edition. Ch. 53: Cultural Agencies. https://www.cato.org/cato-handbook-policymakers/cato-handbook-policy-makers-8th-edition-2017/cultural-agencies (Accessed 10 January 201]8.

Koostra, Barbara (ed.). (2000) *The National Endowment for the Arts, 1965–2000: A Brief Chronology of Federal Support for the Arts*. Washington, DC: Office of Communications, National Endowment for the Arts.

Lewis, Gregory B., and Arthur C. Brooks. (2005). A Question of Morality: Artists' Values and Public Funding for the Arts. *Public Administration Review* 65 (1): 8–17.

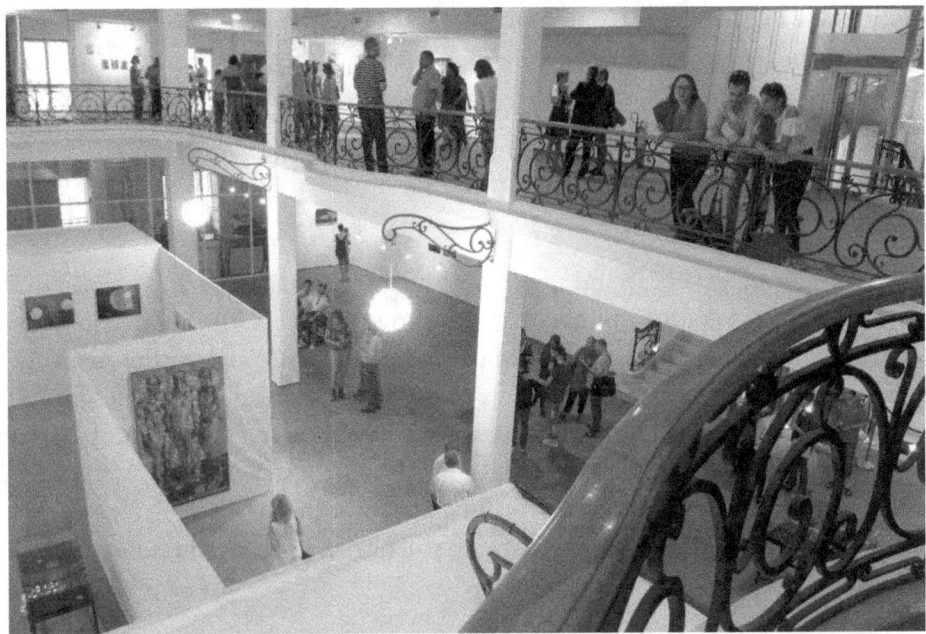

Figure 1: Photo credit Anne Murray. Museum of Modern and Contemporary Art of Oran

EXODUS: A MIRROR OF HOPE FOR THE FUTURE OF ART BIENNIALS

ANNE MURRAY

Anne Murray is both an American and Irish artist, who works with video poetry, sound, and interactive installations. She holds a Master of Fine Arts and Master of Science in Theory, History, and Criticism of Art and Architecture, Pratt Institute, New York, a Master of Education in Teaching English to Speakers of Other Languages from The College of New Jersey Global Studies Program in Mallorca, and a Bachelor of Fine Arts from Parsons School of Design in Paris. She lives and works in Barcelona.

Interview by artist and participant Anne Murray[1] with the two curators and co-founders of the Mediterranean Biennial of Contemporary Art of Oran, Algeria,[2] Sadek Rahim[3] and Tewfik Ali Chaouche, President of Civ-Oeil Gallery.[4]

---

[1] http://www.annemurrayartist.com/

[2] http://biennale-artcontemporain-oran.e-monsite.com/

[3] http://cloudconversations.weebly.com/sadek-rahim.html

[4] http://www.civoeil.com/

4th Mediterranean Biennial of Contemporary Art of Oran, Algeria,
(4éme Biennale Méditerranéenne d'Art Contemporain d'Oran)
July 2–31, 2017
Museum of Modern and Contemporary Art of Oran/MAMO[5]

Today's mixture of classic and unconventional biennials has been exploring where we are going globally in terms of art, its movements, and its connections to globalization. The curated sections of this year's Venice Biennale at the Arsenale and Giardini focused more on texture, form, and color rather than politics, while some of the individual pavilions handed out unique passports and visas such as the Tunisian Freesa and the NSK pavilion passport. Although these ideas are not new, since it was Jorge and Lucy Orta who gave out Antarctica World Passports at the 9th Shanghai Biennale back in 2012, they are an indication that artists are still challenging the viewer and the world of politics.

Recently, such avant-garde approaches to the biennial format as the Museum of Non-Visible Art Biennial (MONA Biennial), The Wrong (biennale),[6] which combines digital pavilions with physical exhibitions around the world, and the Worldwide Apartment and Studio Biennial[7] have created a different context all together for the purpose and venue of a biennial in contemporary times. The United States has seen a rise in interest in Islamic art with the displays at the Museum of Modern Art being changed over to represent Islamic art in the collection as a protest to travel bans[8] as well as the active collecting happening with the important Guggenheim UBS Map Global Art Initiative,[9] which has expanded the collection to include more artists from South and Southeast Asia, Latin America, the Middle East and North Africa. In Spain, the recent exhibit, *Making Africa*, showed at the CCCB, Center of Contemporary Art of Barcelona,[10] and represented artists and designers from all over Africa, and was a more than subtle hint at the necessity of constructing a vision of Africa of the future through art. Still in Venice, we had a limited amount of representation from Africa and its diaspora with the Diaspora Pavilion, including some key emerging artists and mentor artists of influence from multiple diasporas, and the Nigerian (for the first time), Egyptian and South African Pavilions.

The Mediterranean Biennial of Contemporary Art of Oran, Algeria, which is in its fourth edition this year, is entitled, Exodus, and is themed from the heart, refusing to indulge in

---

[5] https://www.founoune.com/index.php/mamo-musee-dart-moderne-contemporain-doran-ouvre-portes-21-mars-2017/

[6] http://thewrong.org/The-Wrong-biennale

[7] http://www.wasbiennale.com/

[8] https://www.nytimes.com/2017/03/18/autossell/proposed-travel-ban-at-art-dubai-its-plainly-wrong.html

[9] https://www.guggenheim.org/map

[10] http://www.cccb.org/es/exposiciones/ficha/making-africa/213052

the mass of political ambiguity and safe quadrants of benign titles and approaches, but instead confronts directly the global issues of exodus as well as "innovative" interpretations of exodus as a concept. Artists have created works about exodus referring from everything to the exodus from Syria to exodus as a drug trip. I asked the curators, Sadek Rahim and Tewfik Ali Chaouche, a few questions via email about the exhibition's development, challenges and the direction it is heading toward, in terms of creating a solid contemporary lift-off for Algerian artists and an Algerian pavilion in the future.

Murray: What were the last three biennials like? What venues? How many artists? How were they selected?

Ali Chaouche: The three previous biennials were at the Oran Cathedral (Médiathèque). The 1st Biennial theme was *Contemporary Art in Every State* and it took place from November 27–29, 2010. There were 30 artists who participated hailing from four countries, with 120 works of plastic art and 30 videos. We had 1200 visitors, and it was curated by Hachemi Ameur, Director of the Fine Arts School of Mostaganem.

The 2nd Biennial theme was *Young Contemporary Creation* and it was from March 29–31, 2012 with 50 artists, of whom 15 were foreigners. We had two artists-in-residence: Samta Benyahia and Flaye. There were 3,000 visitors and I was the curator.

The 3rd Biennial theme was *The Other* and it was from June 8–10, 2014, also with 50 artists including 15 foreigners and we also had the same two artists-in-residence: Samta Benyahia and Flaye. We had less visitors that year because the timing was during the Baccalaureate exams, around 1,500 visitors. We also had an art intervention by the collective BOX 24 (Algiers) and a video projection, a selection from the international festival *Five*. The curator was Karim Sergoua (artist/teacher at the Fine Arts School).

Murray: How do local artists feel about the Venice Biennial? Is it a goal to be represented there?

Ali Chaouche: The Venice Biennial remains the principal frame of reference for excellence for every artist in the Mediterranean region and, most certainly, for Algerian artists in their quest for international recognition, knowing full well that after having exposed their work in the "oldest biennial of the world" its fame will move an artist further up the list of notoriety; some of the artists who have benefited from this recognition and opportunity are French-Algerians, who have had the opportunity to show in other national and curated pavilions, which are not labeled as Algerian, thanks to the help of their galleries, examples are Kader Attia and Adel Abdessemed.

Murray: Sadek, as an Algerian artist with growing distinction in the world, especially after your recent participation in Art Dubai, what are your thoughts and goals and are they related in any way to the Venice Biennial?

Rahim: Even though one's chances are slim, with my gallery owner in Algiers, Amal Rougab, and the president of the Biennale of Oran, Tewfik Ali Chaouche, we are setting up a project and hoping that the Ministry of Culture will finally make a contribution to try to have a space in the next edition of the Venice Biennale. We are very motivated since for a very long time artists of Algerian origin participated in the Venice Biennial under so many other flags other than the Algerian one: Kader Attia, Zineb Sedira, Samta Benyahia ... in 2015 Massinissa Selmani presented with curator Okwui Onwezor the project *All the world's future* which had a "Special Mention" during the 56th Biennale of Venice.

Murray: What are some of the similarities and connections between Venice and Oran historically and in contemporary times?

Ali Chaouche: Oran and Venice are both Mediterranean cities, which have experienced a rich history of cultural and artisanal exchange since the time of the Ottoman empire, when the governor of Oran, Mohamed Kebir, employed some Venetian artisans for the decoration of his palace and vice versa, some Andalusian artisans from Oran, passed their knowledge and skills to Venice. From previous Venice Biennials, one has seen some connections made to Algeria in the French pavilion, most notably with the architecture in the balconies of the architect Pouillon (from the period of colonization).

Murray: What is it that attracts Algerian artists to the Venice Biennial, is there an interest in its connection to the art market?

Ali Chaouche: The Venice Biennial is the tipping point of contemporary art; it is of major importance in the world art market with its reputation and above all, it is the meeting place for art enthusiasts and collectors, from which stems the interest of curators and Algerian gallerists to eventually have representation with an Algerian Pavilion in Venice.

Murray: How do you see the attraction of Algerians to the Venice Biennial and what are some of the issues related to the contemporary art scene in Algeria that you see manifesting themselves?

Rahim: Many artists leave Algeria because there is a great lack of galleries, museums, art fairs and above all the art market here is at its very infancy. Most of these artists leave the country for Europe or the USA, like Yazid Oulab, Massinissa Salmani or Adel Abdessemed. Artists who are still in the country bet on international events to show their work, to make a living and especially to prove to all the world that there is a consequent art production in the country. So, events such as the Venice Biennial are the ideal opportunity for Algerian artists to prove themselves and their very artistic existence.

Murray: The development of national pavilions has been a large part of the history of the Venice Biennial, how does that relate to Algeria historically and the desires of Algerian artists?

Rahim: In Algeria since its independence in 1962, protectionism, populism and above all nationalism are strict in the country; I wonder how the Algerian state resisted an opportunity like the Venice Biennial to show its power and greatness as is often done during military parades and other nationalist occasions.

Murray: What makes the biennial in Oran distinct from other biennials in the world?

Ali Chaouche: It's the people and the city, who are open to Mediterranean cultures and to the world, the people are welcoming and curious about contemporary art. On the economic plane, Oran is the second largest city in Algeria after the capital, with its oil port of Arzew and its industrial zone; it has been in a state of urban expansion since 2010 and there is an awareness that it is still in an adolescent stage (with the formation of new networks of roads and urban spaces, etc.) ... from this, the interest springs to create a new contemporary art space, like the Museum of Modern and Contemporary Art of Oran, where the biennial is held this year, and for the work of the organizers of the creation of the network of art lovers and emerging collectors, businessmen like Mr. Dillali Merhi, who owns a collection of Dinet, which he donated a part of it to the Royal Hotel of Oran, an art space where many art enthusiasts who are investors in Oran in the domain of art and culture can meet up; it is a city that flourishes day by day with its youth population very focused on new mediums of contemporary expression (photo, video, installation).

Murray: What makes this year's biennial in Oran important?

Ali Chaouche: In our eyes, the 4th edition of the biennial in Oran is important because it confirms how unique this union of contemporary art of the Mediterranean is; unique because it is created by an artistic and cultural association (Civ-Oeil Gallery). For this reason, one can not simply compare it to other biennials that are run by state authorities and ministries (where politics lays a hand on art). Also, another important element of the 4th edition, is the theme, *Exodus*, which tips its hat to humanity, which, in my opinion, remains the center of interest of authentic and sincere contemporary creation. This is especially true with regard to the artists of Mediterranean countries.

Murray: How is Oran influenced by tourism and what does this mean for the role of visual arts professionals?

Ali Chaouche: Yes, it is influenced tremendously by tourism. During the holiday season, 8 million tourists come to enjoy the spas with their natural springs in the city. It is important for visual arts professionals to invest in the creation of galleries and contemporary art exhibition, spaces connected to tourist sites, in order to magnify the exhibitions and festivals in this domain to ensure a creative and dynamic environment, in the sense that it is the tourists, who are in a way the ones who can help launch the art market, as I said before, this implies both art enthusiasts and collectors.

Murray: Why do it? What makes you put the time in to create a large-scale exhibition like this in Algeria?

Ali Chaouche: Civ-Oeil Gallery was created in August 1997. For 20 years, we have, myself and some other founding members, organized the 1st National Salon of Fine Arts of Oran. In 2000, we followed with several editions in partnership with the director of culture of the city of Oran, but our ambition grew beyond the scope of the Mediterranean in 2005, and since then many countries have participated. The 5th Mediterranean Salon of Fine Arts was a complete success in terms of artistic exchange and culture, and let's not forget to mention that at the time we organized, simultaneously, the Mediterranean Salon of Visual Art and the International Rai Festival of Oran (another level of sharing between visual artists and musical artists). In 2010, we decided to create this biennial, thankfully with the encouragement of many partners, who have promised us their help (it is only that we had some financial problems relating to our commitments, which are neutral and non-political). We maintain our freedom in our choices and ideas with respect to the founding principles of the Democratic and Popular Republic of Algeria. Our biennial is founded and created by an artistic and cultural association independent of any guardianship. In the end, what really brings us to realize the magnitude of the impact and importance of this biennial, is our success in the previous editions, which makes our commitment to sharing and creating exchanges between other countries and artists of the Mediterranean and the world, a key factor in creating a message of peace for a better world.

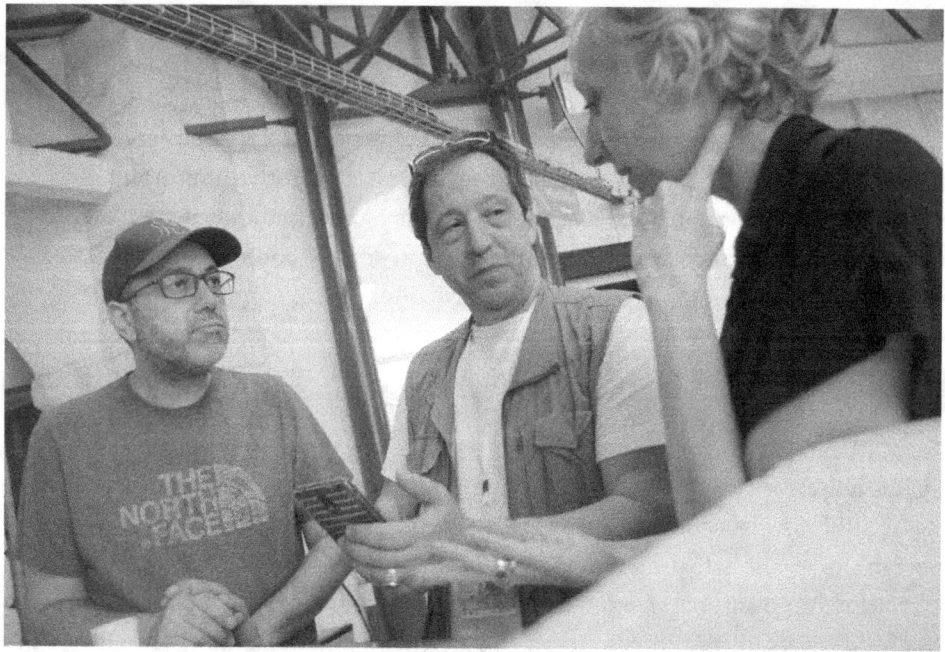

Figure 2: Photo credit Anne Murray. Curators Sadek Rahim (on the left),
Tewfik Ali Chaouche, and journalist Stéphanie Pioda

Murray: What did you expect from artists who submitted work for the theme of exodus?

Ali Chaouche: There were 37 Algerian artists and 20 foreign artists this year, hailing from England, Canada, Spain, France, Syria, Switzerland, Turkey, Tunisia, Palestine, the United States, Greece, Italy and Thailand and the exhibition took place at the recently inaugurated Museum of Modern and Contemporary Art of Oran. The participating artists, who submitted their work for the theme of exodus, were welcomed as a part of this project, because of their human and artistic engagement: as was stated in the open call for the theme, "Art is the mirror of society; it reflects one's daily life happiness and sadness." The works of these artists echo this reflection to the public. For me, my objectives as a curator were to re-introduce contemporary art to the people of Oran who could not see and frequent exhibitions and visual art events for a long time except at the Civ-Oeil Gallery, which shows contemporary art of Oran from time to time; there are no other visual art exhibition spaces in Oran and in the region for that matter.

Murray: Similarly to the early days of the Venice Biennale, I noticed that the biennial in Oran included a selection of invited artists, open call artists selected from around the world, and emerging Algerian artists. Is this the way that the selection was made in the past or was it a new combination this year? Was there a particular reason why you made the grouping this way this time?

Ali Chaouche: Concerning the selection of artists, this year, we opted to have three invited Algerian artists who have been recognized recently for their creative productions and their diverse exhibitions across Algeria and abroad. The other artists who were chosen represent all the different cities of Algeria, and some of the Mediterranean countries. We accepted some countries outside of the Mediterranean region because of their relationship to the theme of exodus.

Murray: Sadek, what was your major role as a curator in this exhibition? I understand that you worked with several of the young artists helping them to develop their ideas, what can you share with us about this experience? In the Diaspora Pavilion in Venice, they paired more established artists with emerging artists to help build and support the younger artists and their careers. Do you think this combination will be a new trend in biennial exhibitions? How do you see what you did in relation to the pairing of artists in the Diaspora Pavilion? As an established artist yourself, were you acting as curator and mentor to these young artists?

Rahim: What David A. Bailey and Jessica Taylor have done, as curators of the Diaspora Pavilion in Venice, and which is very interesting, is to create a pavilion structured as a project. They had the great idea to put out an open call for emerging British artists of various backgrounds in 2016. These young artists had not only to work for projects for the biennial but also a 2-year agenda of mentoring and support by a group of established artists. What we wanted to do at the Mediterranean Biennial of Contemporary Art in Oran was a bit the same, except with regard to Algeria; there is a sense of urgency, because we are significantly behind in this area.

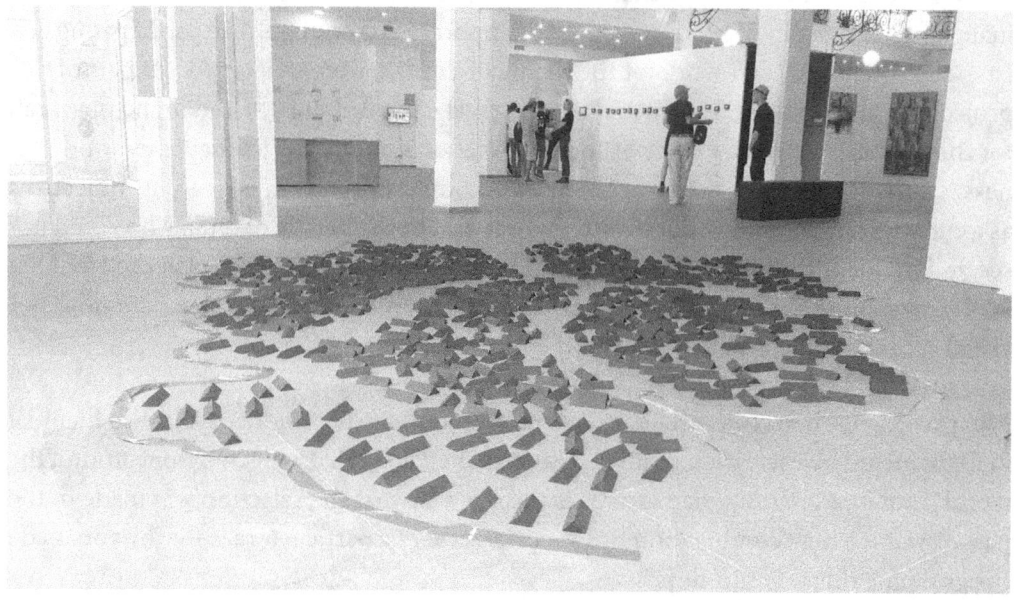

Figure 3: Photo credit Sadek Rahim. *Camps*, an installation by Djamel Benchenine[11]

My curatorial work with these three young artists was such a great experience as an artist and as a supporter of change in the cultural and academic programs of our country. These artists: Islem Haouti, Nora Zaïr and Djamel Benchenine were such a good example of what we can do to help young artists to take a step forward. Djamel Benchenine had proposed at the end of my work with him, an installation 6/7 meters called "Camps" a model of a Sahrawi refugee camp (Dakhla) in the city of Tindouf in Algeria. He made the tents of this camp out of wood, originally white, but later he painted them in black, a color that reflects the tragedy of these people's lives. In 2016, Djamel was invited as an artist to The International Film Festival of Western Sahara (Fisahara[12]), which takes place at this camp among others and also, simultaneously, in Madrid, allowing for a greater number of personalities from the world of Spanish cinema culture as well as Spanish citizens sympathizing with the Saharawi cause, and to the public in general, to attend and to inquire about the situation of the Saharawi refugees.

---

[11] https://www.facebook.com/bnchnart/

[12] http://fisahara.es/?lang=en

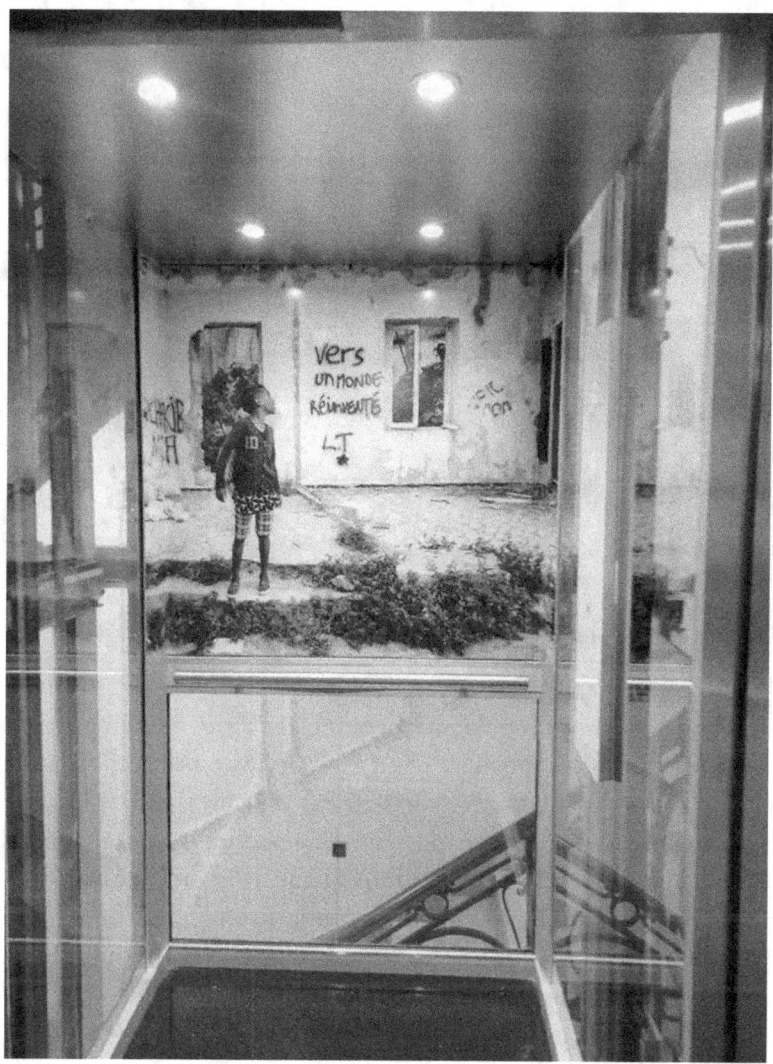

Figure 4: Photo credit Nora Zaïr. A photograph by Nora Zaïr called *Up*

Nora Zaïr, photographer, worked on Rumi poetry. Rumi was one of the first who elaborated the "Sufi turning" or the dervish dance, the physical exertions of movement, specifically dancing and whirling, in order to reach a state assumed by outsiders to be one of "ecstatic trances" a way to travel "above" to be closer to heaven. Her installation, a photograph "big sticker" is glued to one of the panels of the museum elevator. Nora photographed a kid next to graffiti on a wall, which said "towards a reinvented world."

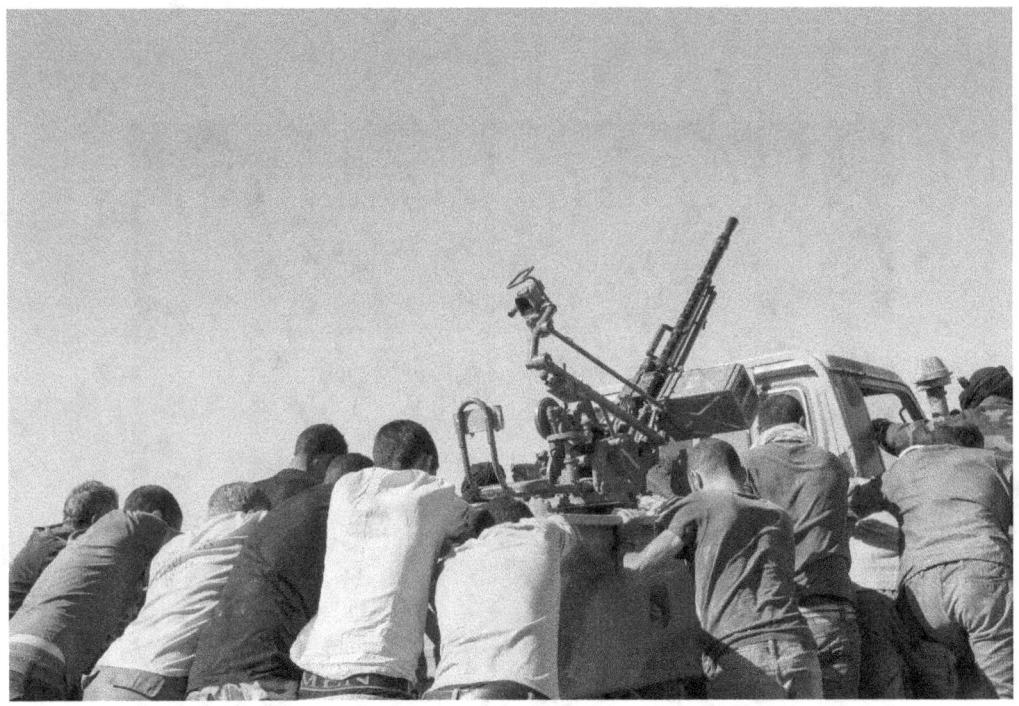

Figure 5: Photo credit Islem Haouti. *Freedom* by Islem Haouti

My work with photographer Islem Haouti was mostly about contemporary techniques and how to represent photography in a contemporary way. Islem chose to print a photograph called "freedom" taken in the Western Sahara camps on a sticker and directly mounted it on one of the walls of the museum. The picture was taken when he worked with the Spanish human rights organization ARTifariti,[13] inside a camp in the Western Sahara in 2016. And finally, yes, I think this combination should be a trend in the biennials, especially those of the Arab world and more precisely of the MENASA region (Middle East, North Africa and South Asia).

Murray: Who were the main jury members for the selection and what background do they have? Have they been involved with this biennial since the beginning?

Ali Chaouche: The principal members of the jury were Sadek Rahim,[14] artist master's laureate of the world-renowned, Central St. Martins University of the Arts in London, and co-curator and co-founder of the Mediterranean Biennial of Contemporary Art of Oran; Hafid Boualem, filmmaker and screenwriter (member of Civ-Oeil Gallery); Karim Benacef, journalist (director of publication); Abdelhamid Aouragh, photographer (journalist for Elkhabar); and myself, President of the Jury, artist (co-founder and president of the Mediterranean Biennial of Contemporary Art of Oran). During the 3rd

---

[13] http://www.artifariti.org/en/

[14] https://www.saatchiart.com/account/profile/90542

and 4th biennial, I was the curator representing Algeria in the Magmart International Videoart Festival. The members of the jury are all members of the Association of Visual Arts, Civ-Oeil, and they have participated actively in the preparation of the 4th biennial. In the role of co-curator, I consulted many professionals in the field of contemporary art concerning the choices for the 4th biennial (outside of the jury itself), and with Sadek Rahim we made a final selection taking into consideration the context of contemporary Algerian artists, integrating the works of some young emerging artists, who were included at the end with the selected artists.

Murray: What particularly surprised you about the submissions this year?

Ali Chaouche: This year, many artists surprised us with the context of their works:

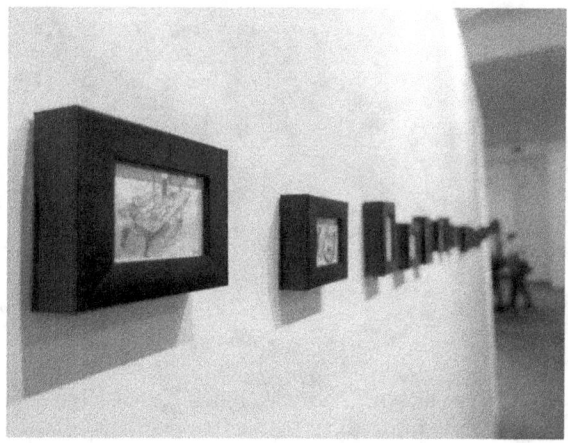

Figure 6: Photo credit Djamel Benchenine.
Installation *Exodus Cigarette* by Djamel Benchenine

Benchenine Djamel with his installation *Exodus Cigarette*: this recent graduate of the Fine Arts School of Oran made a connection with the younger generation of artists searching for liberty and discovery, he started by making graffiti on the walls of Oran (he draws, paints and writes poetry to express himself and communicate a message) ... with this installation, he delivers to us a strong and expressive message of exodus in relation to cigarettes (youth smoke Kif or hashish for their specific exodus) ... through these drawings on cigarette papers, he tells us of the daily life of all youth who are forgotten in the shadows of the exodus of the cigarette. Benchenine cites three stages of the drug trip for young people: first trip toward God (with the worst and the best ... to meditate), second is a trip across Europe (immigration or exile), third a trip through the cigarette papers (his drawings on these little translucent papers, but it is also a trip into recklessness from the effects of hashish used to forget all of life's daily problems).

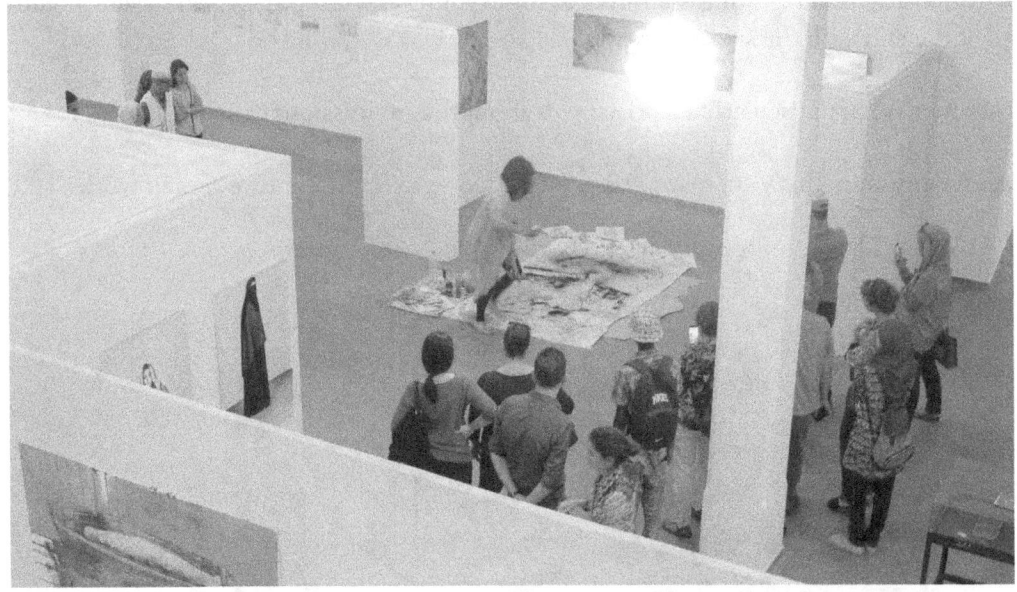

Figure 7: Photo credit Tewfik Ali Chaouche. Artist Reyna (Renée Rey) performing *Les Naufragés* at the Mediterranean Biennial of Contemporary Art of Oran

Renée Rey (Reyna)[15] This French artist is personally engaged in the theme with her performance art connecting photo-video and installation with paintings of drowned people; she presents to us a different way of participating in a biennial of contemporary art, where her way of sharing with the public of Oran engages the audience quickly. Her section at the exhibition was the most visited and achieved the greatest interest and curiosity from the public.

---

[15] http://reyna-art.net/

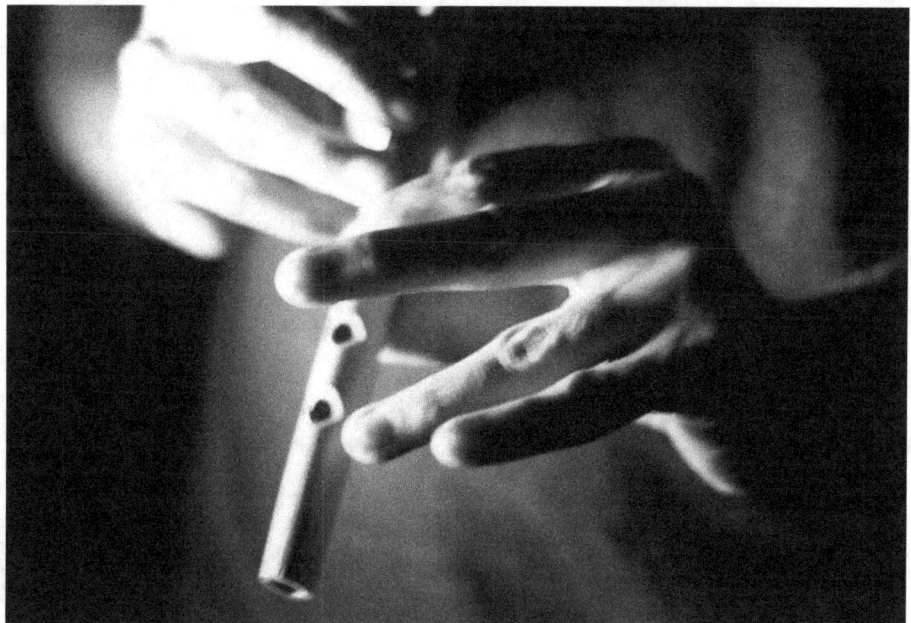

Figure 8: Photo credit Sofiane Zouggar. *Stories/Moving Objects* by Sofiane Zouggar

Sofiane Zouggar[16] A young contemporary Algerian artists presents his reflection on exodus through a work entitled, *Stories/Moving Objects,* a beautiful story of a Syrian refugee from Aleppo, exiled to Algiers through the melodies of reed instruments that he makes and plays ... this video shows us the drama of the Syrian exodus from a different artistic angle with musical harmonies of the Ney (an oriental flute made of reeds).

Murray: Were there unexpected interpretations of the exodus theme?

Ali Chaouche: Yes, there were some artists whose works interpreted the theme of exodus in a very different way that is what makes contemporary art so rich, the video art was more present in this biennial, a new thing for the MAMO, which was recently inaugurated in March 2017 and did not always have the technical requirements for video projection. As an American and Irish artist, and global citizen, your work was quickly noticed for your beautiful performance video and photo installation highly enhanced by the technique and style of the interpretation of the theme of exodus, which takes a dimension more psychological in the video accompanied by a narrative text ... I see it as a professional work, which makes us proud to have you among the selected artists.

---

[16] www.sofianezouggar.com

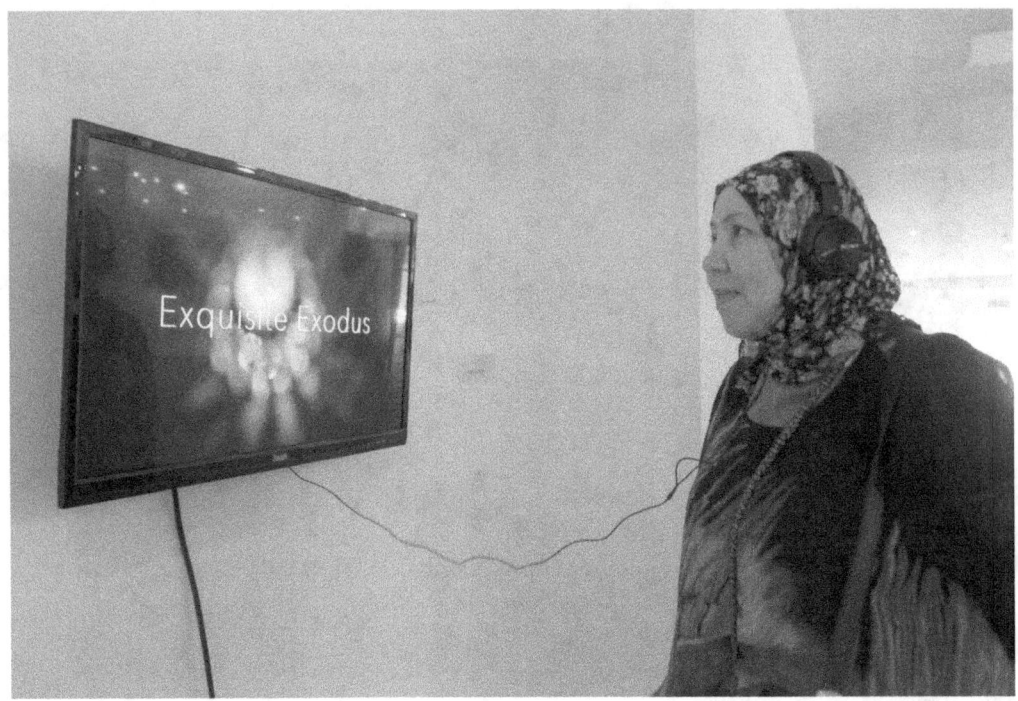

Figure 9: Photo credit Anne Murray. Fellow artist participant, Sihem Salhi, watching the video *Exquisite Exodus*[17] by Anne Murray

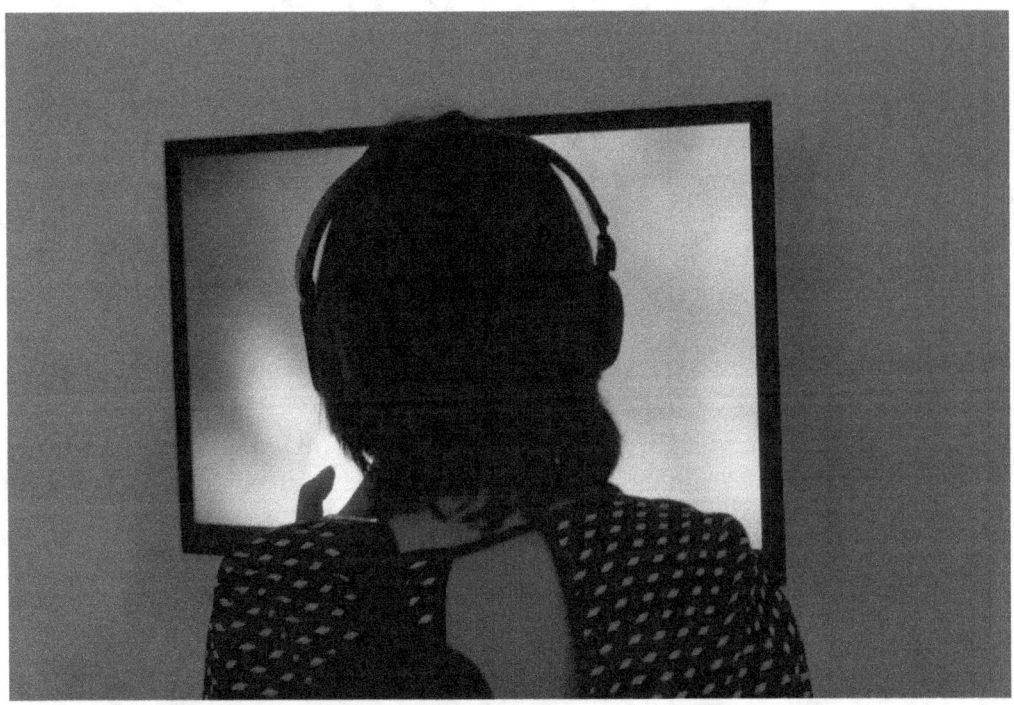

Figure 10: Photo Credit Anne Murray. Video *Exquisite Exodus* by Anne Murray

---

[17] Watch the video here: http://www.annemurrayartist.com/exquisite-exodus.html

Murray: What do you plan for the upcoming biennial?

Ali Chaouche: Everything depends on finances. If our association sustained financial support from the ministry of culture for this event, it would have been different: we would have an open call to find an event agency that could create the programming for this international event a year in advance. We would choose three independent professional curators, with each proposing a different theme: 1 curator for the Algerian diaspora abroad, 1 curator to choose the local artists and 1 curator to choose the foreign artists. The biennial would extend to other spaces around the city of Oran and we would create a catalogue before the opening of the exhibition and other brochures to share around the city and to attract tourism. There would also be guided visits for students and scholars with mediators of contemporary art.

Murray: How much do you think the venue and the support of the organizations involved has affected the outcome of the biennials of the past and the current biennial?

Ali Chaouche: Without a doubt, the place of exhibition and the support of state institutions plays a crucial role in the continuation of this art event: previously we had no financial support from the Ministry of Culture, and yet, thanks to various sponsors and partners, we were able to mount this biennial anyway (in the basement of the Mediateque (former Cathedral of Oran, which is currently empty). Now with the new Museum of Modern and Contemporary Art, the director is in favor of a partnership and so the financing for the next edition is open to possibilities and we have an optimistic vision for the future.

Murray: Tewfik, what do you as a curator and/or artist bring to the biennial that is unique?

Ali Chaouche: As the curator and artist founder of this biennial, I do everything I can with the organization, administration, and the making of the different exhibitions. There are multiple objectives for this biennial: to create a platform of contemporary art for exchange between artists of the Mediterranean region; also to create an Algerian art market in partnership with the international art market; to make the work of contemporary Algerian artists known internationally, to participate in the confrontation of some of the themes that unite us and, finally, to participate in the evolution of contemporary art in the Mediterranean region with conferences and round tables, as well as to create catalogues and brochures.

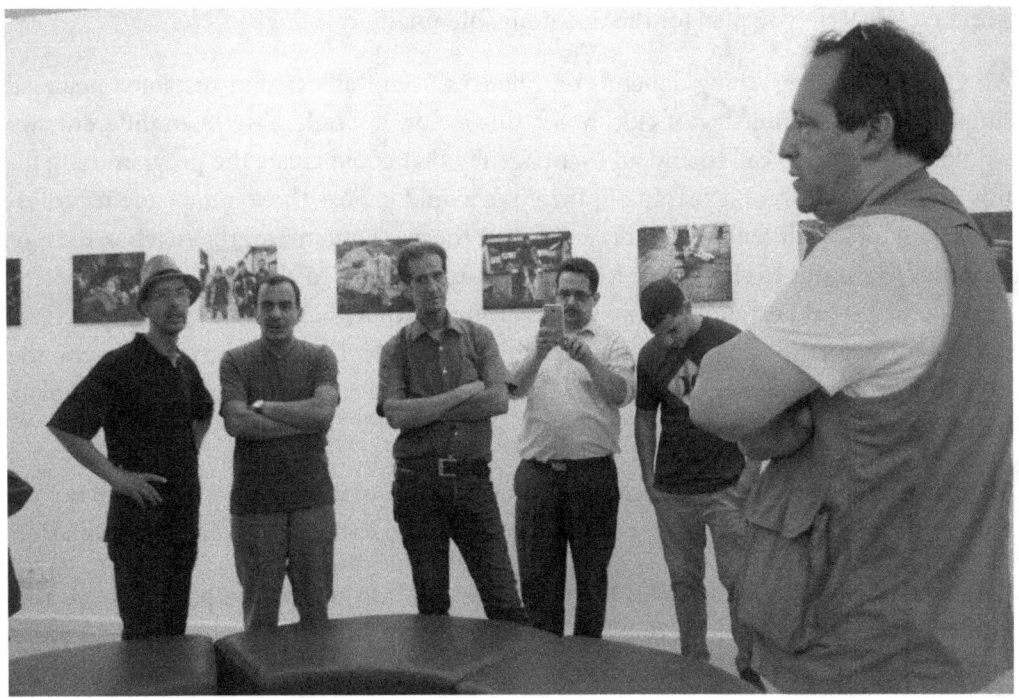

Figure 11: Photo credit Anne Murray. Guided visit with curators and artists
to the Institut Français of Oran

Murray: I also want to mention that there were great things happening for both the public and the participating artists in the biennial. Several of the artists gave artist talks and also met and interacted with the other artists, including going on a guided visit with both of you to an exhibition at the Institut Français.[18] There were poetry slam events, musical events and author events. Congratulations to you both on a very successful biennial with such tremendous attendance on a daily basis from the public!

---

[18] http://www.if-algerie.com/oran

THE SCALES, POLITICS, AND POLITICAL ECONOMIES OF CONTEMPORARY ART BIENNIALS

JULIA BETHWAITE

Faculty of Management, Degree Programme of Politics,
University of Tampere, Tampere, Finland

Julia Bethwaite is a Doctoral Student in International Relations in the Faculty of Management, University of Tampere, Finland. Bethwaite explores the role of art in international relations with a focus on Russian actors in the transnational field of art. She examines practices of cultural diplomacy, transnational cultural relations and the interaction of state and non-state actors within the field of art.

ANNI KANGAS

Faculty of Management, Degree Programme of Politics,
University of Tampere, Tampere, Finland

Anni Kangas is a University Lecturer in International Relations and acts as the Academic Director of the Master's Programme in Leadership for Change in the Faculty of Management, University of Tampere, Finland. Her research interests are in the role of art and popular culture in international relations and the impact of urbanization on world politics. Her research dealing with these issues has been published in Geopolitics, Global Networks, Journal of International Relations and Development and Millennium: Journal of International Studies.

ABSTRACT

The number of contemporary art biennials has increased significantly over the last 25 years giving rise to the phenomenon of biennalization of contemporary art. In this article, we detail the world politics of biennalization through a review of mainly academic literature on biennials. We analyze internal definitions within the reviewed material through three dimensions: scale, politics, and production of value (political economies). Our analysis shows the world politics of biennials revolves around a set of productive tensions between the order of nation states and its alternatives, cultural dominance and resistance, and various modes of value production.

Introduction

Contemporary art biennials are large-scale, high-budget international group exhibitions recurring every two to five years. Their number has proliferated rapidly especially over the last 25 years. There are now estimated to be some 150 such exhibitions taking place in more than 50 countries (Filipovic et al. 2010; Vogel 2010; Sassatelli 2016a). Marchart (2010 [2008]) has come up with the notion of biennalization to refer to the proliferation and standardization of contemporary art exhibitions under the biennial format. Arguably, biennials now constitute a key context through which contemporary art is encountered and experienced. They attract considerable amount of international attention and are seen to provide a setting for surveying trends in "cutting-edge art" (Sassatelli 2016a:1). Biennials are often grandiose and dispersed across several locations in a city. They are locally embedded but usually "global in ambition" (Filipovic et al. 2010:13).[1]

This article probes into the world politics of biennials through an analysis of academic and scholarly materials where biennials are analyzed and debated. On the surface level, the discussion seems polarized. Some argue that the proliferation of biennials can turn contemporary art into a genuinely "global" phenomenon. In their view, biennalization can open up new kinds of spaces of resistance, diversity, reflection, and cross-fertilization of ideas. It can lead toward more democratic redistribution of cultural power (e.g. de Duve 2007:681).[2] Others consider biennalization as a proof of the capacity of neoliberal globalization and culture industry to standardize and instrumentalize contemporary art subjugating its autonomy to demands of political and economic convenience (e.g. Stallabrass 2004; de Duve 2007:684–687; O'Neill & Wilson 2010). In this article, we seek to

---

[1] There are obviously significant differences among biennials but they also share a significant set of traits: commitment to a cosmopolitan perspective combined with efforts to articulate the particularisms of their host cities; financing by mostly public or private sources which are not usually directly dependent on art investors, which gives biennials a "public" character (as compared to art fairs, for example); groundedness upon an idea or concept expected to be communicated by the curators (Kompatsiaris 2014:78). For an articulation of differences among biennials, see e.g. Bydler's (2004:151) classification of three types of biennials: capitalist-philanthropic enterprises initiated at the turn of the twentieth or mid-twentieth century (e.g. the Venice Biennale); events originating in the post-Second World War setting and marked by bloc politics or "underdevelopmentalist" reactions (e.g. Documenta and Münster); and biennials characterized by "event orientation" and "flexible production" in the 1990s and 2000s (e.g. Manifesta).

[2] Panos Kompatsiaris is one among scholars who suggests viewing biennials as attempts to create new worlds. They offer spaces for knowledge production and social criticism, often merge elements of political and social activism into their agendas and may also involve "non-artistic" actors such as "activist groups and marginalized communities" (Kompatsiaris 2014:85). This highlights the potential of biennials to serve as discursive sites for questioning the existing structures and challenging hegemonies. However, this is far from an uncomplicated argument and, as Kompatsiaris also notes, it is pertinent to ask what kind of worlds biennials produce and for whom. Biennials can also be examined as a "lifeblood of contemporary capitalism" engaging with neoliberal economic models and serving the neutralization and institutionalization of the critique (Kompatsiaris 2014:77, 81).

move beyond this opposition. We first detail how scholars and commentators see space to matter to the politics of art biennials. We show that multiple spatialities are implicated in the discussions and debates. To name just a few, biennials are seen to negotiate between the national, global, mobile, and universal. Such spatialities are co-implicated not only with each other but also with different understandings of politics: representation, contestation, hegemony, and empowerment. We argue that understanding the world politics of biennials requires appreciating this co-implication (cf. Leitner et al. 2008).

We have structured our review essay in the following way: We first examine how biennials are scaled[3] in scholarly discussions. We discuss the embeddedness of biennials into the Westphalian spatial order but also highlight a productive tension between the order of nation states and its alternatives, which has been a long-standing element of biennial practices. We also scrutinize arguments according to which biennials are—or have a potential to be—a genuinely global phenomenon as well as suggestions that the notion of "glocalization" best captures the scalarity of contemporary art biennials. From there, we move on to a more explicit discussion of the politics of biennials framed in terms of whether biennials are bound to remain an instrument of cultural domination, a reproduction of the hegemonic—or whether they can fulfil the often-heard promise that biennial art is able to open up new kinds of spaces of resistance, diversity, and reflection. This leads us to a discussion of the political economy of biennials, i.e. to the question of types of value that biennials produce.

Scaling the Biennials

One of the key axes of analysis in the politics of contemporary art biennials is their scalar order.[4] We use the notion of scale to refer to the discursive framing of sociospatial orders, such as local, regional, national, and global (e.g. Delaney and Leitner 1997). In this section of our review article, we examine the scaling of biennials, i.e. the kinds of sociospatial orders into which biennials are embedded in the scholarly literature. We detail the tensions between the order of nation states, globality, g/locality, and universalism in the debates and discussions on biennials.

The Nation and its Discontents

Art biennials have had and continue to have an intimate connection to the national scale. Lawrence Alloway's characterization of the Venice Biennale—the oldest and best-known contemporary art biennial—revolves around nations and national imaginaries:

---

[3] The scale can be understood to refer to a simple hierarchy of nested scales (akin to International Relations' levels-of-analysis discussion). Here, however, we have in mind the idea of scales not as something that pre-exists societal activity but rather as something that is produced in and through societal activity, notably practices of spatial differentiation. Such activity, in turn, produces and is produced by spatial or geographical structures of social interaction. Given this, production of scale is also a potential site of political struggles, which makes it pertinent for discussions of spaces of social justice (Smith 1992:62).

[4] A biennial denotes an exhibition, which occurs once every two years. The Italian word "Biennale", with a capital letter, is often used in relation to Venice Biennale, the oldest art biennial in the world.

The pavilions in the Giardini ... are erected by each country and the styles are a vivid array of national self-images. ... The Hungarian pavilion is folkloric ... , so is the Soviet pavilion. ... The classical styles are all highly indicative of their countries. ... The American pavilion is Colonial neoclassic [... and ...] the Danish pavilion sharp and austere. (Alloway 2010 [1969]:140)

The fact that he—as well as others—has chosen to highlight the role of nations in discussions of biennials is not surprising.[5] In contrast to group shows organized by artists' associations or art museums, invitations to participate in the biennials not only in Venice but also in Cairo, São Paulo, and New Delhi were, for a long time, sent through diplomatic channels to national representatives of specific states. State representatives, such as the Foreign Office or the Ministry of Culture, appointed national commissioners who then selected artists. As a result of this, biennial participation was also taken to reflect the status of a state in international relations (Vogel 2010:7). The institutional history of biennials thus ties them firmly to the Westphalian framework of nation states, diplomacy, and international relations.

However, the framing of biennials in national terms is not only a matter of their institutional set-up. Analyses of biennials often take up the idea of nations competing against each other. They may characterize these events as the "Olympic Games of the Art World" (Sheikh 2010 [2009]:153; see also Sassatelli 2016a:5; Baker 2010 [2004]:450–451). This association is strengthened by the fact that founding of the Venice Biennale took place in close temporal proximity to the founding of two other events based on the idea of competition among nations: the first "world expo" (1851) and modern Olympic Games (1896) (Vogel 2010:17). The framing of biennials as elements in international competition may also take place through defining biennials as "a tribune, on which to represent power" (Bertelé 2013:45), or characterizing art presented there as "an ambassador" (Vogel 2010:8). Jeannine Tang (2007:248) claims that today's biennials remain useful in competitive geopolitical games among states; in Tang's definition, biennials present "ample opportunities for constructing or revising dazzling national representations for cultural competition, as the exhibitions may also combine forces to mobilize regionalism and stake out territory in an internationalized art market" (ibid.).

Characterizing the biennial as a site of national representation is another way of scaling biennials to the context of nations and their representations. This often involves questions such as who is eligible to represent a nation and what kind of art has the right to demonstrate a nation's cultural competence. Sarah Scott's analysis of Australia's participation at the Venice Biennale is an example of this approach. There was a 20-year gap in Australia's attendance at the Biennale after its first participation in 1958. Scott argues

---

[5] However, Shearer West's analysis of the first eleven editions of the Venice Biennale (1895–1914) shows that while the event was intended as an "international" exhibition, the exhibitions actually represented traditional regionalism and biennale activities were focused on enhancing the image of Venice and increasing flows of tourism and commerce (West 1995:413).

that this illustrates a struggle of finding a consensus about how contemporary art should represent the nation. In the 1950s, the Australian Contemporary Art Society saw the Venice Biennale as an opportunity to "increase Australia's links with the international art scene" (Scott 2003:59). But while the Biennale's nature as "a platform for nationalist aspirations and for establishing the canon of each respective country's art" was acknowledged, the status of abstract art as a vehicle of national representation was contested. Being too international, contemporary art was seen to lack "distinct national flavor" (Scott 2003:62).

Today, it is common for artists and other art world actors to explicitly take distance from national framings. The concept of national representation is also being increasingly problematized in practices and discussions surrounding biennials. In 1994, Manifesta—the "roving European Biennial of Contemporary art"—emerged to problematize place-boundedness and to map out a "new cultural topography" in the aftermath of the Cold War (Manifesta www document; Filipovic 2014:50). The 26th edition of the São Paulo biennial was framed as a critique of national representation and an attempt to attain "freedom from the great geopolitical machine ruling cultural bureaucracy" (Lagnado 2006:17; see also Vogel 2010:7). Some scholars, however, insist that the framework of nations and states should not be ignored in analyses of biennials. Chin-Tao Wu, for example, claims that it is still possible to interpret the national pavilions at the Venice Biennale in relation to the geopolitical power of various countries (Wu 2007:381; see also Rodner & Preece 2016). A similar claim is voiced by Tang, according to whom the institutional privileging of powerful states is a defining feature of the Venice Biennale. The Biennale's curatorial rhetorics often resonate with postcolonial critiques and are full of intentions to level cultural hierarchies. However, the less powerful countries with temporary pavilions are still situated farther away from the valuable locations, such as the main entrance. As Tang notes, this "defines visibility within a field of competing national representations, as most visitors ultimately view pavilions close to the main venue" (Tang 2007:253).

The way in which the concept of national representation is simultaneously reproduced and problematized through biennial practices is a focal point of much of current research on biennials. As Caroline A. Jones aptly suggests, biennials are an enlightenment project, which "secures a kind of nationalism in the act of transcending it" (Jones 2010:76). Although it has become common to claim that the national pavilion system of the Venice Biennale is obsolete, nations remain central. The concepts of nation are needed at the same time as the "desire for the world picture" prompts subjugating terms such as "nation" and "internationalism" to critique (Jones 2010:83; see also Basualdo 2010 [2003]:129). Chu-Chiun Wei's (2013) analysis of the changing curatorial strategies of the Taiwanese pavilion—or collateral event—also shows the character of contemporary art biennials as a flexible mechanism. They both reproduce and reject the modernist idea of nation states. Rafal Niemojewski highlights that biennials vary in their relationship to the world of nation states. Founded as a "celebration of the nineteenth-century idea of the nation state", the relationship of the Venice Biennale to the world of nation states is different from that of the Havanna Biennial, for example. La Bienial de la Habana was born in the context of historical transformations associated with globalization (Niemojewski 2010:99–100). Its stated departure from the frame of the nation state is also reflected in its practices: For example, the artworks are displayed according to formal criteria, not according to national origin. In the exhibition catalogue, the artists are arranged in alphabetical order, not by nationality (Niemojewski 2010:96).

From International to Global

As the above examples show, some scholars continue to emphasize the importance of nations and states in the politics of biennials. At the same time, it is increasingly common to critically evaluate the national and international aspects of biennials and contemporary art. This may involve, for example, foregrounding the idea that the biennial institution is "at its core, global" (Filipovic et al. 2010:22) or pointing out that art, by character, is transnational or post-national.

Several scholars argue that the development of the biennial institution, and especially the proliferation of biennials in different parts of the world, offers evidence of a move away from the Westphalian imaginary toward a "unified, transnational institution of art" (Carroll 2007:138). In contrast to artistic exchange occurring *across* different art world institutions—such as Japanese theater and European theater—Carroll sees contemporary art as an internally coherent practice with a shared language, tradition, and sense-making strategies: conversational presuppositions, hermeneutical gambits, recurring themes, and sense-making strategies.[6] At today's biennials, Carroll argues, artworks deriving from nominally different cultures, stand side by side, play related language-games and share the same traditions of interpretation (Carroll 2007:141). According to Marian Pastor Roces (2010 [2005]:55), this is not a new phenomenon. In fact, a spatial discourse of the global was part of the universal expositions that can be treated as the predecessors of the biennials. Both the Venice Biennale and the Expos had universal ambitions in the sense of being tied to the idea of humanity's progress.

Contemporary art biennials may also be argued to have an active role in creating alternative world orders. Boris Groys, for example, suggests that biennials have a specific role to play in today's world where capitalism operates globally, but there is no global political project. In these conditions, biennials offer a terrain on which models for a new global order can still be envisaged and imagined (Groys 2009:64–65). Working with the Kantian idea of *sensus communis*, de Duve also sees biennials as a mechanism able to surpass local specificities; there is potential for "aesthetic cosmopolitanism" in them. Esthetic cosmopolitanism would be a form of cosmopolitanism that is founded esthetically, not

---

[6] Carroll (2007:141) exemplifies this with the idea that urinating into the Tate Modern's version of *Fountain*, Yuan Cai and Jian Jun Xi may or may not have been aware of Pierre Pinoncelli urinating into another version of *Fountain* in Nimes. However, both were able to make a gesture as they were tapping into the tradition of Duchamp.

politically. It utilizes the idea of universality and universally shared feelings and agreements, and takes place in negotiations concerning the label of art and esthetic judgments (de Duve 2007:684–685).

> [Kant] grasped that an issue of such magnitude as peace on earth was at stake in a sentence so anodyne as "this rose is beautiful". When replaced by "this cultural product is art", the real depth of his thinking on aesthetics comes to the fore. (de Duve 2007:686).

Another way of addressing the global character of contemporary art biennials is presented in Nadine Siegert's analysis of the Luanda Triennial. Siegert's analysis takes place against the background of Becker's well-known idea of an "art world", which is constituted by individuals (and organizations) who contribute to the production of works of art while being dispersed around the world (Siegert 2014:176). Siegert points out that such a conception of the international art world has tended to exclude the Global South: the proliferation of the biennial institution across the world does not guarantee mobility and interaction in equal measure for all. Today's art world "consists of a number of smaller, locally embedded art scenes, each with very different histories and dimensions" (Siegert 2014:176). It is thus global in the sense of being a decentered and pluralized entanglement or assemblage. As Siegert emphasizes, it is important to pay attention to the intertwining of the global and local and the resulting political dynamics when discussing the "globalization" of biennials. Interestingly, Siegert discovers that the idea of national reconstruction and representation has played a crucial role when biennials—e.g. the Cairo Biennial, Dak'art, Rencontres de Bamako, and Johannesburg Biennale—have been founded on the African continent. For example, at the same time, as the actors involved with the Luanda Triennial aspire to "global participation" and seek recognition from the "international art world", the exhibition has had an important role in negotiating and reconstructing the decolonized, postwar Angolan society, and its relation to the world. The Luanda Triennial, while avoiding the concept of national art, remains in many ways tied to the key notions and images of Angolan patriotism and nationalism (Siegert 2014:188). Siegert's analysis thus illustrates an important point about biennials more generally: a variety of sociospatial orderings matters and different spatial framings are productively intertwined in the politics of biennials.

Biennials as an Instrument of Cultural Domination

The way in which biennials are scaled is closely related to the question of their politics, i.e. whether and how biennial practices produce and reproduce existing power relations and serve as mechanisms of cultural domination. In other words, the scales of biennials are co-implicated not only with each other but also with different understandings of politics: contestation, resistance, dissent, hegemony, and empowerment. In this section of the review article, we detail this aspect in the world politics of biennials.

Replicating Cultural Hegemony through Biennials

There is a wealth of literature debating whether it is possible to contest existing power relations through biennials. Filipovic (2014) argues that although biennials claim to offer a counter model to the modern, Western museum institution, they replicate some of its questionable paradigms. Despite aiming to decenter the traditional notions of modernity and give voice to underrepresented cultures, histories, and politics, they most often end up replicating the Western museum's frame—the white cube. Arguably, such homogenization is paradoxical. It goes to the heart of the neoliberal model of globalization against which many biennials seek to position themselves:

> [N]o matter how fervently biennials and large-scale exhibitions insist on their radical distinction from the idea of the museum, they overwhelmingly show artworks in specially constructed settings that replicate the rigid geometries, white partitions, and windowless spaces of the museum's classical exhibitions, that is, when biennials are not simply bringing artworks into existing museums without altering their white cubes. Timeless, hermetic, and always the same despite its location or context, this globally replicated white cube has become almost categorically fixed, a private "non-place" for the world of contemporary art biennials, one of those uncannily familiar sites, like the department stores, airports, and freeways of our period of supermodernity described by anthropologist Marc Augé. (Filipovic 2014:48).

It is, indeed, quite common to claim that biennials—the Venice Biennale in particular—play a role in replicating the cultural hegemony of the West or Global North (e.g. de Duve 2007:681). The logic of this argument often is that having emerged as part of the modernizing, civilizing, or colonizing projects of the Global North (or West), it is quite impossible for biennials to escape this legacy. Marian Pastor Roces suggests that although an "attempt to outstare the colonizer's gaze" forms part of the shift toward global art events, these are still "spaces of contest that mirror the spaces created by the forces contested". She is thus sceptical that spaces that were produced in the nineteenth century for the global diffusion of capitalist power could be converted into spaces for social justice (Pastor Roces 2010 [2005]:53–54; see also Bakshtein 2015:394). In a similar tone, Valerie Kabov argues that the Venice Biennale represents the "northern version of the seeing and representing the world." In opposition to the Global South and "emerging markets", it is tied to "Northern views, needs and agendas" (Kabov 2016:1). Kabov comes to this conclusion through an analysis of the Venice Biennale as a mechanism for emerging countries to seek validation from the Global North. She suggests that the Venice Biennale is a seemingly democratic system that recites postcolonial critiques in its curatorial rhetorics, but in reality supports and reproduces the existing power relations and inequalities on the global scale. The Global North still has the power to decide what gains recognition (Kabov 2016:3–5).

A related claim is that the popularity and expansion of contemporary art biennials does not signal the emergence of a decolonialized, democratic, and global art world. Chin-Tao Wu argues that the biennials embody "the traditional power structures of the contemporary Western art world; the only difference being that 'Western' has quietly been replaced by a new buzzword, 'global'" (Wu 2009:115). In this interpretation, hegemonic power is at play in the mutually shared agreement to obey the established conventions of the biennial institution. In a similar way as Kabov, Wu argues that the "culturally dominated" feel the need to be present at biennials in order to have their identity recognized (Wu 2007:385).

Sites of Resistance and Dissent

In contrast to arguments that biennials cannot avoid reproducing cultural hegemony, some scholars see possibilities for resistance in them. Rafal Niemojewski, for example, highlights the need to foreground the significant differences among biennials. While some biennials may indeed be seen to reproduce existing power structures, others do provide a site for "promoting peripheral art scenes as part of the global circuit" (Niemojewski 2010:95). Niemojewski problematizes the commonplace treatment of the Venice Biennale as the hegemonic form to which other biennials should be traced. He foregrounds the role of the Havana Biennial as the "most important point of reference for the contemporary biennial" (Niemojewski 2010:101; see also Basualdo 2010 [2003]:128). In this interpretation, the establishment of the Havana Biennial in 1984 marked a new turn in biennial history; it established the biennial as the platform for the critique of the modernity that the biennial institution can be argued to have sprung from (Niemojewski 2010:100). "By focusing on creating horizontal connections (South-South) that provide alternatives to the art routes inherited from modernity the Havana Biennial enabled a new type of global exhibition that debunks the myths of teleological modernity and explores the plurality of modernism" (Niemojewski 2010:100). However, the capacity of the biennial institution to provide an alternative to the existing institutional frameworks within the contemporary art world is a question that, according to Niemojewski, remains open (Niemojewski 2010:101).

As economic and cultural hegemony has been one of the often-discussed subjects among the scholars and representatives of the art world, it has also inspired opposed actions. For some, the utopian promise of the biennial has been, and is, the promulgation of counter-narratives and experimentation with counter-models (Filipovic et al. 2010:23). For Filipovic, biennials remain a site of ambiguity, inquiry, and experimentation, a critical site of experimentation. They offer counterpoints to the regular programming of the museum and other traditional art institutions, platforms for addressing politically charged issues as well as eliciting a questioning of artistic practices (Filipovic 2014:47; see also Basualdo 2010 [2003]:124–135; see also Hoskote 2010:308). Paul O'Neill argues that it has been through providing platforms for critical discussion and recognizing wider audiences that biennials have been able to provide models of resistance to the hegemony of established art institutions and Western art history (O'Neill 2012:85; see also Marchart 2013).

Thus, for many scholars the fact that biennials have been firmly tied to hegemonic structures does not mean that it would be impossible to use them to advance other agendas. Okwui Enwezor claims that biennials are still able to expose the limits and contradictions of Western epistemologies. Being aware of the fact that an expansionist mode of biennials has given rise to a negative impression of biennials as "an agora of spectacle" (Enwezor 2010 [2010]:434), he claims that biennials may enable a transformation of spectatorship toward a less possessive direction (Enwezor 2010 [2010]:441). Enwezor is thus among the scholars claiming that the "globalization" of the phenomenon of biennials can be made to signal a process of fragmentation and that this can unhinge totalizing notions of art and culture. Understood in the wider context of feminism, multiculturalism, liberation theology, resistance art, queer theory, and rights of indigenous peoples, the hegemonic concept of spectatorship becomes fragmentary and is replaced by the idea of "general spectatorship", which is tied to neither the logic of the nation state nor that of imperialism (Enwezor 2010 [2010]:442–444).

Curiously, participation at the Venice Biennale can be interpreted as a counter-hegemonic act as such. An example of this is offered in Wei's analysis of the Taiwanese pavilion. After being symbolically diminished from the status of an official national pavilion to a collateral event at the Venice Biennale in 2003, the function of the pavilion changed. Instead of representing Taiwanese art and making the public familiar with Taiwan, representing a "critical perspective" became the main function of the Taiwanese unofficial, self-proclaimed pavilion (Wei 2013:475–481). In Wei's words, it "critiques the logic of cultural, political and economic hegemony dominating the biennale and caus[ing] Taiwan's own marginality", acting as a device of critical globalism (Wei 2013:483). Arguably, the case of the Taiwanese pavilion shows that the non-Western participants and the "oppressed" are not passive, hegemony-obeying victims, but can also use the existing structures to advance their own agendas[7] (Wei 2013:474–484).

From the point of view of an analysis of the politics of space of contemporary art biennials, Simon Sheikh's interpretation of the possibility of biennials to function as sites of resistance is particularly interesting. Sheikh recognizes that a residue of national myth-making and production of citizenry is at work in biennials and that they are intimately tied to processes of capital accumulation. However, he claims that things start to look different if we examine them through the prism of interconnectedness—the sense of any place being always seen in relation to another place, or a series of possible places: "What goes on 'here' always has effects 'there', and vice versa, even when we are not aware of these movements. ... [O]ne of the characteristics of advanced art is precisely that it allows one to see more than one viewpoint: more than one story or situation, and

---

[7] In short, relational understanding of space suggests that types of associations and relations between entities precede identities (Massey 2005).

more than one way to look at them" (Sheikh 2010 [2009]:158). Working with such relational understanding of space (e.g. Massey 2005), Sheikh approaches biennials through the category of the heterotopia. They are "capable of maintaining several contradictory representations within a single space" (Sheikh 2010 [2009]:163). Heterotopia allows for the fact that while biennials are part of hegemonies, mechanisms for generation of monopoly rent or city branding, this does not mean that they need to affirm such hegemonies. They can be made to signify differently: "It is improbable that a biennial can exist without taking part in … processes of capital accumulation (both symbolic and real, of course), so the question is rather, can they do something else simultaneously?" (Sheikh 2010 [2009]:163).

Cultural Political Economy of Biennials

An important dimension in the world politics of biennials is their cultural political economy, i.e. the question of the kind of value that is produced at biennials. There are two interlinked dimensions to this discussion: The first reviews contributions examining the biennial phenomenon in the context of post-Fordist processes of capital accumulation and search for monopoly rent through exclusivity. The second takes up the character of biennials as badges of distinction and mechanisms of accruing not only economic but also symbolic capital (Bourdieu 1983).

Some scholars highlight the fact that the oppositional value of contemporary art has been suppressed namely as exchange value considerations have taken over. The embeddedness of contemporary art biennials in the search for monopoly rent has implications for the capacity of biennials to function as spaces of justice and to realize their stated goal to bring into being liberating "new worlds" (Basualdo 2010 [2003]; Kompatsiaris 2014). Panos Kompatsiaris discusses the contradictions that emerge when a biennial's ideological agenda—e.g. social criticism toward the neoliberal economic model—collides with their practices of funding and hiring labor, for example: "One must necessarily begin by asking what kinds of worlds are these institutions capable of producing and more importantly for whom" (Kompatsiaris 2014:77, 82–86). Filipovic, van Hal, and Øvstebø also suggest that the increasing dominance of the place-branding agenda in biennial operations has lent legitimacy to the claim that the word biennial stands for little more than "an overblown symptom of spectacular event culture" (Filipovic et al. 2010:13). Biennials are argued to instrumentalize the symbolic value of art which flows from art's presumed autonomy from the market logic (Basualdo 2010 [2003]:129–130) and characterized as commercially driven showcases akin to Disneyland (Filipovic et al. 2010:13). Tang suggests that biennials function as "tastemakers, mobilized to reinforce certain politics through aesthetic representation" while being smoothly integrated into "capital's flows and political status quos" (Tang 2007:258).

Money has, indeed, always played a role at biennials, and a strand of the literature on biennials focuses on its implications for the politics of biennials. One of the primary goals of the Venice Biennale when it was established in the late nineteenth century was to establish a market for contemporary art. In 1968, the ban on sales was established as a result of student protests that saw the Biennale as a site for the commodification of culture (see also Jones 2010:79). Despite this, several analysts note that it is difficult to distinguish contemporary art from various kinds of economic circulations. This is the case especially taking into consideration the financialization of contemporary art and the consolidation of the figure of the "art investor" (e.g. Coslor 2016). The Venice Biennale plays a specific role in building momentum for art as an investment class. "Showing in Venice speeds up sales, gets artistic careers going, cranks up price levels and helps artists land a dealer ranked higher in the market's hierarchy," as Olav Velthuis argues (Velthuis 2011:22). This "Venice effect" is built on a paradox: due to its noncommercial nature, the Venice Biennale enables demonstrating one's independence from the market and autonomous interest in art. However, this symbolic capital can be easily converted into economic capital: "So the paradox is that the curator's resistance to commerce and Venice's official status as a non-selling event is exactly what makes its quality signals influential in the art market" (Velthuis 2011:23).

In addition to the Venice effect on the art market, there is some discussion in the existing literature on the influence of funding and corporate sponsors on what is exhibited at biennials (e.g. Grace 2015; Kabov 2016). Robert Grace, for example, points out while the ratio between governmental and private funding varies considerably between the participating pavilions at the Venice Biennale, corporate funding is often involved. The motivation of such funding for contemporary art is generally based on the logic of commercial exchange, which has implications for the autonomous status of art. Grace illustrates this with the example of a major sponsor of the French pavilion at the Venice Biennale in 2015, who set a condition to serve beer produced by one of his companies at pavilion's vernissage (Grace 2015:25–26). Valerie Kabov has also scrutinized the influence of funding on the politics of biennials. She remarks that in the case of private and NGO funding, the paths often "run along colonial and neo-colonial lines" molding the artists from the "emerging countries" according to the needs of the Western funders (Kabov 2016:4–5). When this is combined with the limited ability of governments from the global south to support the costs of mounting national pavilions at the Venice Biennale, their ability to participate remains dependent on the imperatives of northern funders: "What this unambiguously suggests is that participation of Southern artists in Venice Biennale will continue to be is filtered to tune of Northern money and Northern audiences" (Kabov 2016:4).

The economic dynamics of biennials are not always as straightforward as the question of how the funding of biennial activities is tied to attempts to further specific interests. More complex economic processes are also at play. Two strands of discussion can be distinguished here: one focuses on the connections of biennials to processes of capital accumulation and the other on their role in the accumulation of symbolic capital. One of the scholars who have tried to tie their analyses of biennials to wider circuits of capital and mechanisms of capital accumulation is Panos Kompatsiaris. He highlights that the proliferation of biennials has to be examined in the context of *post-Fordist processes of capital accumulation*. While the extraction of surplus value was tied to the production site under Fordism, in post-Fordism its extraction becomes diffused in the sphere of the circulation of capital in the financial, touristic, and cultural sectors—"the seeking of valorization in collective desire ... has been capital's response to the problem of growth" (Kompatsiaris 2014:81; see also de Duve 2007:682, Sheikh 2010 [2009]:155).

Monica Sassatelli's work provides a counter argument to claims of the logic of commodification dominating biennials. Sassatelli has pointed out that analyzing biennials in terms of the logic of commodification is reductionist in the sense of, firstly, hiding the specificities of symbolic production and, secondly, positing economic value and value of art as "hostile worlds" (Sassatelli 2016a:4). Instead, Sassatelli promotes an analysis of biennials in terms of the "symbolic production of art". This approach is able to take into account questions of value production without explaining everything away using the logic of commodification. The notion of the "symbolic production of art" stands for the process of valuation rendering a work, an artist, or a genre relevant and appreciated. In this capacity, biennials mediate between "the constitution of aesthetic dispositions and the legitimation of regimes of meaning and value" (Sassatelli 2016a:3; see also O'Neill 2012:72). In terms of politics of space, an analysis of the symbolic production of art could imply keeping a closer eye on ongoing struggles and searches for new rationales for what is actually valued and what is not (cf. Sassatelli 2016a:13).

Conclusions

In this review article, we have reflected on the world politics of contemporary art biennials. Three key dimensions emerged from our analysis: scale, politics, and value. Scale refers to the sociospatial ordering of biennials. Politics stands for the question of whether biennials reproduce or challenge existing power relations, and value refers to the ways in which not only economic but also symbolic capital is produced in and through biennials.

Analyzing scholarly articles on biennials, we have shown that a significant amount of practices of and academic discussion on biennials takes place around the question of scale. Scholars writing about biennials often depart from the relevance of nations and national representation and propose alternatives to it. There is, indeed, a productive tension between the order of nation states and its alternatives—the global, local, or glocal—within biennial practices as well as in commentaries on them. There are also suggestions that such relational notions as heterotopia or assemblage would best capture the spatiality of biennials. This shows that a variety of sociospatial orderings matter for the politics of contemporary art biennials. Multiple spatialities and scales are relevant in order to understand the politics of space of contemporary art biennials. There is no need to privilege any of them but rather to pay attention to their co-implication, e.g. to the way in which they intersect and influence each other.

As to the politics of biennials, we have discussed the capacity of biennials to offer models of resistance, expose contradictions within epistemologies, and provide platforms for countering various forms of dominance. We have also detailed claims according to which biennials tend to reproduce hegemonies through their art practices and political economies. Probing the biennials' cultural political economies, we showed that they are intimately linked to the dynamics of capital accumulation and production of monetary value within the current capitalist model. However, not only economic but also symbolic, cultural as well as political capital, can be generated through biennials. They can thus be connected to other regimes of value than commercial value. The idea of multiple, co-implicated spatialities and ways of being political also suggests that the persistence of national framings or hegemonic connections does not mean that biennials cannot be something else at the same time. Foregrounding such heterotopic character of biennials can also offer a way out of polarized interpretations, which see biennials *either* as global spaces of diversity and resistance *or* as examples of the way in which neoliberal capitalism commodifies culture.

Acknowledgements

The research for this article was made possible by funding from the Kone Foundation and the Academy of Finland (project number 298883). The authors would like to thank the members of the research project Spaces of Justice Across the East-West Divide and participants of the Tampere Security Research Group (TASER) as well as the editors and referees of the AIA Journal for insightful comments on the manuscript.

References

Alloway, Lawrence. (2010 [1969]) The Biennial in 1968. In *The Biennial Reader,* eds. Elena Filipovic, Marieke van Hal, and Solveig Øvstebø, 136–149. Ostfildern: Hatje Cantz.

Baker, George. (2010 [2004]) The Globalization of the False: A Response to Okwui Enwezor. In *The Biennial Reader,* eds. Elena Filipovic, Marieke van Hal, and Solveig Øvstebø, 446–453. Ostfildern: Hatje Cantz.

Bakshtein, Iosif. (2015) Sovremennoe Iskusstvo i Ego Proekty. Biennale i Vokrug. In *Vnutri Kartiny. Stat'i i Dialogi o Sovremennom Iskusstve,* 389–394. Moscow: Novoe Literaturnoe Obozrenie. [Бакштейн, Иосиф. (2015) Современное Искусство и Его Проекты. Биеннале и Вокруг. In Внутри Картины. Статьи и Диалоги о Современном Искусстве, 389–394. Москва: Новое Литературное Обозрение.]

Basualdo, Carlos. (2010 [2003]) The Unstable Situation. In *The Biennial Reader*, eds. Elena Filipovic, Marieke van Hal, and Solveig Øvstebø, 124–135. Ostfildern: Hatje Cantz.

Bertelé, Matteo. (2013) From Stateless Pavilion to Abandoned Pavilion. Russia and the Soviet Union in Venice, 1920–1942. In *Russian Artists at the Venice Biennale 1895–2013*, 44–51. Moscow: Stella Art Foundation.

Bourdieu, Pierre. (1983) The Field of Cultural Production, or: The Economic World Reversed. *Poetics* 12 (4–5): 311–356.

Bydler, Charlotte. (2004) *The Global Artworld, Inc. On the Globalization of Contemporary Art*, 151. Uppsala: Uppsala Universitet.

Carroll, Noel. (2007) Art and Globalization: Then and Now. *The Journal of Aesthetics and Art Criticism* 65 (1): 131–143. Special Issue: Global Theories of the Arts and Aesthetics.

Coslor, Erica. (2016) The Financialization of the Art Market. *E-International Relations*. <http://www.e-ir.info/2016/03/01/the-financialisation-of-the-art-market/> (Accessed 10 November 2017).

de Duve, Thierry. (2007) The Glocal and the Singuniversal. Reflections on Art and Culture in the Global World. *Third Text* 21 (6): 681–688.

Enwezor, Okwui. (2010) Mega-Exhibitions and the Antinomies of a Transnational Global Form. In *The Biennial Reader*, eds. Elena Filipovic, Marieke van Hal, and Solveig Øvstebø, 426–445. Ostfildern: Hatje Cantz.

Filipovic, Elena. (2014) The Global White Cube. *oncurating.org* 22: 45–63. <http://www.on-curating.org/index.php/issue-22-43/the-global-white-cube.html> (Accessed 29 February 2017).

Filipovic, Elena, Marieke van Hal, and Solveig Øvstebø. (2010) *The Biennial Reader*. Ostfildern: Hatje Cantz.

Grace, Robert. (2015) Australian Pavilion Venice. *Architecture Australia* 4: 20–27. <https://architectureau.com/articles/australian-pavilion-venice/> (Accessed 20 December 2017).

Groys, Boris. (2009) From Medium to Message. The Art Exhibition as Model of a New World Order. *Open 2009, The Art Biennial as a Global Phenomenon* 16: 56–65.

Hoskote, Ranjit. (2010) Biennials of Resistance: Reflections on the Seventh Gwangju Biennial. In *The Biennial Reader*, eds. Elena Filipovic, Marieke van Hal, and Solveig Øvstebø, 306–321. Ostfildern: Hatje Cantz.

Jones, Caroline A. (2010) Biennial Culture: A Longer History. In *The Biennial Reader*, eds. Elena Filipovic, Marieke van Hal, and Solveig Øvstebø, 76–83. Ostfildern: Hatje Cantz.

Kabov, Valerie. (2016) *The Role of the Venice Biennale Partnership with the Art Market in Real and Perceived Democratization of the Art World – African Contemporary Art Case-study in the Context of the Global South.* Paper presented at IESA conference 'The Venice Biennale and the Art Market, the Venice Biennale as an Art Market: Anatomy of a Complex Relationship', London, February 3–5 2016.

Kompatsiaris, Panos. (2014) Curating Resistances: Ambivalences and Potentials of Contemporary Art Biennials. *Communication, Culture & Critique* 7: 76–91.

Lagnado, Lisette. (2006) Introduction. In *27a. bienal de São Paulo*, 16–18. São Paulo: Fundação Bienal de São Paulo.

Leitner, Helga, Eric Sheppard, and Kristin M. Sziarto. (2008) The spatialities of contentious politics. *Transactions of the Institute of British Geographers* 33 (2): 157–172.

Manifesta www-document. About the Biennial. <http://manifesta.org/biennials/about-the-biennials/> (Accessed 11 January 2017).

Marchart, Oliver. (2010 [2008]) Hegemonic Shifts and the Politics of Biennialization: The Case of Documenta. In *The Biennial Reader*, eds. Elena Filipovic, Marieke van Hal & Solveig Øvstebø, 466–491. Ostfildern: Hatje Cantz.

Marchart, Oliver. (2013) The Globalization of Art and the Biennials of Resistance. In *CuMMA Papers* 7. Helsinki: Aalto University. <https://cummastudies.files.wordpress.com/2013/08/cumma-papers-7.pdf> (Accessed 20 December 2017).

Massey, Doreen. (2005) *For Space.* London: SAGE.

Niemojewski, Rafal. (2010) Venice or Havana: A Polemic On the Genesis of the Contemporary Biennial. In *The Biennial Reader*, eds. Elena Filipovic, Marieke van Hal, and Solveig Øvstebø, 88–103. Ostfildern: Hatje Cantz.

O'Neill, Paul. (2012) Biennial Culture and the Emergence of a Globalized Curatorial Discourse: Curating in the Context of Biennials and Large-scale Exhibitions since 1989. In *The Culture of Curating and the Curating of Culture(s)*, 51–85. Cambridge, MA: The MIT Press.

O'Neill, Paul, and Mick Wilson. (2010) Introduction. In *Curating and the Educational Turn*, eds. Paul O'Neill and Mick Wilson, 11–22. London: Open Editions.

Pastor Roces, Marian. (2010 [2005]) Crystal Palace Exhibitions. In *The Biennial Reader*, eds. Elena Filipovic, Marieke van Hal, and Solveig Øvstebø, 76–83. Ostfildern: Hatje Cantz.

Rodner, Victoria L., and Chloe Preece. (2016) Painting the Nation: Examining the Intersection Between Politics and the Visual Arts Market in Emerging Economies. *Journal of Macromarketing* 36 (2): 128–148.

Rogoff, Irit. (2006) The Art Biennial Geo-Cultures: Circuits of Arts and Globalizations. *Open!* <https://www.onlineopen.org/geo-cultures> (Accessed 3 February 2017).

Sassatelli, Monica. (2016a) Symbolic Production in the Art Biennial: Making Worlds. *Theory, Culture & Society* 34 (4): 89–113. DOI: 10.1177/0263276416667199.

Sassatelli, Monica. (2016b) The Biennalization of Art Worlds: the Culture of Cultural Events. In *Handbook of The Sociology of Art and Culture*, eds. Laurie Hanquinet and Mike Savage, 277–289. London: Routledge.

Scott, Sarah. (2003) Imagining a Nation: Australia's Representation at the Venice Biennale, 1958. *Journal of Australian Studies* 27 (79): 51–63.

Sheikh, Simon. (2010 [2009]) Marks of Distinction, Vectors of Possibility: Question for the Biennial. In *The Biennial Reader*, eds. Elena Filipovic, Marieke van Hal, and Solveig Øvstebø, 150–163. Ostfildern: Hatje Cantz.

Siegert, Nadine. (2014) Luanda Lab – Nostalgia and Utopia in Aesthetic Practice. *Critical Interventions* 8 (2): 176–200.

Smith, Neil. (1992) Contours of a Spatialized Politics: Homeless Vehicles and the Production of Geographical Scale. *Social Text* 33: 54–81.

Stallabrass, Julien. (2004) *Art Incorporated: The Story of Contemporary Art.* New York: Oxford University Press.

Tang, Jeannine. (2007) Of Biennials and Biennialists. Venice, Documenta, Münster. *Theory, Culture & Society* 24 (7-8): 240–260. DOI: 10.1177/0263276407084709.

Tang, Jeannine. (2011) Biennalization and its Discontents. In *Negotiating Values in the Creative Industries. Fairs, Festivals and Competitive Events*, eds. Brian Moeran and Jesper Strandgaard Pedersen, 73–93. Cambridge: Cambridge University Press.

Velthuis, Olav. (2011) The Venice Effect. *The Art Newspaper Magazine.* June, 21–24.

Vogel, Sabine B. (2010) *Biennials – Art on a Global Scale.* Vienna: Springer.

Wei, Chu-Chiun. (2013) From National Art to Global Criticism. The Politics and Curatorial Strategies of the Taiwan Pavilion at the Venice Biennale. *Third Text* 27 (4): 470–484.

West, Shearer. (1995) National Desires and Regional Realities in the Venice Biennale, 1895–1914. *Art History* 18 (3): 404–434.

Wu, Chin-Tao. (2007) Occupation by Absence, Preoccupation with Presence: A Worm's Eye-View of Art Biennials. *Journal of Visual Culture* 6: 379–386. DOI: 10.1177/1470412907084514.

Wu, Chin-Tao. (2009) Biennials without Borders? *New Left Review* 57: 107–115.

CITIES ARE DRIVING NEW CULTURAL POLICIES

ANNA LISA BONI
Secretary General of EUROCITIES

Anna Lisa Boni has been secretary general of EUROCITIES since June 2014. Before joining EUROCITIES, she was director of the Brussels office of the French region Provence-Alpes-Cote d'Azur. EUROCITIES is the network of major European cities. It brings together the local governments of over 140 of Europe's largest cities and more than 40 partner cities, that between them govern 130 million citizens across 39 countries.

PHILIPPE KERN
Managing Director of KEA European Affairs

Philippe Kern Philippe is the founder of KEA European Affairs, and has been its managing director since 1999. KEA has been advising territories, organisations and people to unlock the potential of cultural and creative industries since 1999.

Culture is everywhere. It reaches out well beyond museums, heritage sites, or traditional cultural institutions, infiltrating our daily life. It can be found in technology hubs, in media clusters nourishing innovation, on city walls in the form of graffiti and murals, or at local community centers and street festivals which trigger social interactions. It serves to create an aesthetic, an atmosphere, and ultimately the attractiveness of places.

While the analysis of global transformation has begun to stress the cultural dimension, there is a predominance of a particular type of study. The literature is rather focused on technology (digital networks, artificial intelligence, genetic manipulation, the Internet of Things for instance), climate change, population growth, or economic sustainability. This shows a tendency to attribute historical development mainly to economic, technological, business, and demographic factors, as if ideas, creations, institutions, and culture played little role in major global change.

Too often, culture and its agents (artists, creative professionals, cultural institutions) are given poor consideration in the context of economic and social development. This is not new, but rather puzzling, considering the important role of culture and cultural operators in the shaping of today's and tomorrow's world.

The lack of awareness of the transformative power of culture and its ability to address economic, social, or diplomatic issues may be due to various factors:

- cultural administrations are not yet equipped or given the mandate to manage cultural policies in a more holistic way;

- the word 'culture' can carry the stigma of being inefficient, marginal, secondary, or trivial;

- the concept of innovation has been hijacked by technology industries and their powerful lobbying, to the detriment of creation in its more traditional sense, which is actually what innovation is based on;

- cultural stakeholders need to upgrade their lobbying skills and gain confidence and conviction.

Of all public institutions, cities are the most aware of the importance of managing local cultural resources to remain relevant and attractive. Culture is increasingly mainstreamed in various policy areas such as innovation, economic development, social cohesion, urban planning as well as cities' external relations strategies. The Culture for Cities and Regions[1] project, on which the authors met, sought to overcome specific local challenges through targeted peer-learning and study visits between cities to share knowledge and encourage this mainstreaming of culture.

Cultural investment and cultural workers influence the attractiveness of cities, the spirit and morale of people, and are the focus of cultural policies. Such initiatives are often piloted by development or economic agencies as part of innovation programs, often in the social field or as part of urban regeneration. They are also the result of individual or collective initiatives emerging from collaborative ecosystems, which are often enabled by city-level matchmaking, for example between businesses, cultural organizations, or universities. It can also be the direct result of public support for the arts or because of a concentration of active creative personalities and entrepreneurs in one city or area of a city.

As a result, cities are triggering a cultural policy revolution. This trend is due to the increased evidence of the impact of cultural investment on urban regeneration. The new cultural policies are aimed at augmenting or leading local development, and they focus on:

- developing long-term cultural visions and programming at local level;

- occupying former industrial sites with new economic or social activities;

---

[1] Culture for Cities and Regions. (2015) The legacy of Culture for Cities and Regions. www.cultureforcitiesandregions.eu (Accessed 21 November 2017). This three-year project led by EUROCITIES in collaboration with KEA, produced a catalogue of 70 case studies, organized 15 thematic study visits and provided expert coaching for 10 cities/regions. Funded under the EU's creative Europe programme, it aimed to take stock of existing practices all over Europe to exchange and promote transfer of knowledge, to better understand successful cases of cultural investment, and to go into the details of policy planning and implementation.

- making use of heritage buildings that are difficult and costly to maintain;
- attracting creative talents and artists and maximizing the potential for local crafts by making workspaces available at lower costs;
- changing citizens' perceptions of an urban space through artistic interventions to encourage ownership, civic pride, and urban regeneration;
- generating fun and entertainment (well-being and social cohesion) through festivals and cultural events;
- supporting cultural and creative entrepreneurship (incubators, living labs, creative hubs, maker spaces) to support jobs;
- attracting tourism or international investors (cultural events and an attractive suite of cultural infrastructure and reputation as a destination city/region);
- addressing social problems (artistic intervention with focus on enjoyment, self-expression, inter-community and inter-generational dialogue and skills development/training to prevent social exclusion, isolation, and marginalization);
- helping the city to internationalize.

A large number of cities contribute to successfully mainstreaming culture in various policy areas with a view to promoting:

- links between innovation and cultural policy—artists and creatives to encourage innovation across the city, and to encourage this by linking digital and tech hubs with cultural and creative hubs;
- usage of heritage and memory to build self-awareness, self-worth, and social cohesion—this will build strong social values and help combat xenophobia, racism, anti-Semitism, gender discrimination, and extreme nationalism;
- empowerment of people through artist and design-led education, living labs, and co-creation methodologies;
- capacity building to enable quality local cultural expression, audience development, and participation;
- intercultural dialogue and positive, proactive approaches to managing cultural integration,
- fight against social inequality in urban and rural contexts, by stimulating cultural entrepreneurship and better management of local cultural resources to maximize participation and ownership from citizens.

A new urban movement on its way—leading to social transformation

Today, culture (notably through mass media and social media) is key to organizing the communities that make up societies. Artists, creative businesses, designers, architects, technologists, digital aficionados, cultural activists, game developers, archaeologists, and the public are mingling in co-working spaces, fab labs, living labs, maker spaces, creative hubs, and incubators. Together, they are inventing a new society of collaborations and enterprises.

The international community of cultural workers is cosmopolitan with a global mindset. They are concerned about issues such as nationalism, xenophobia, environmental protection, and climate change. However, this sensibility is not preventing pride in their cultural roots and desire to share their stories. Regional cultures (Bavaria, Catalonia, Corsica, Flanders, Scotland) enhance the expression of European diversity and promote democratic participation.

In parallel, the consumption of culture is changing and becoming more focused on shared activities. Events and festivals based around music, street art, theatre, film, spoken word, or food create opportunities for people to get together. Cultural consumption is an excuse to celebrate together. This culture is about making friends and creating more opportunities for sharing. It is about co-producing among peers, and informal or project-based initiatives which are often carried out by independent freelancers working outside corporate settings, but who, at the same time, are in some way connected to such environments.

This trend, this new way of working, favors collaboration as opposed to competition, establishing solidarity and partnerships, and new forms of entrepreneurship driven by social rather than economic goals. It offers a vision of society and its structure, in which the nation state will be one unit of integration among others, but in which cities will co-exist. A societal vision that will be post-capitalist, driven by knowledge, and foresees cultural stakeholders playing a key role in developing a new social ideology based on creativity and innovation. This society might be divided by new sets of values—one promoted by the technologists and scientists, and one by the cultural workers. Creative parks or innovation hubs often group both skills to generate innovation and creativity in an interdisciplinary spirit. Cities have a role to play in encouraging both worlds to converge and collaborate, to enable us to imagine tomorrow's world.

www.ingramcontent.com/pod-product-compliance
Lightning Source LLC
Chambersburg PA
CBHW081302170526
45165CB00011B/3382